This collection is quintessential Kan praise indeed. . . . These pieces are s funny, and a complete pleasure to re.

Scott Turow, Author
Personal Injuries and *Presumed Innocent*

My first thought was, if God is indeed a Cubs' fan, then He has a lot of explaining to do. My second thought was, well, perhaps in this instance, team members and followers should be guided by the Book of Job.

There is a legitimate theological issue here, to be sure, and Arnold Kanter puts his finger on its pulse. (A pulse, by the way, being something only a handful of Cubs players over the years have demonstrated they possess).

Ira Berkow
Sports Columnist, *New York Times*

Filled from cover to cover with wit, wisdom, and heart—and you don't have to be Jewish or a baseball fan in order to enjoy it. . . . Arnie Kanter is the consummate tour guide for the glorious heartbreak that is Cubs baseball.

Rabbi Brant Rosen
Jewish Reconstructionist Congregation
Evanston, Illinois

The tougher it gets for Cubs fans, the more beer I sell—and Arnie's been one of my best customers for years.

Bob Chicoine,
Wrigley Field beer vendor and poet

You have just accomplished what we both thought would be utterly impossible: You have displaced Dave Barry on our nightstand, and we'll be reading about the Cubs at bedtime for the foreseeable future. I'm glad you brought that team to our attention. It had escaped our notice until now, but then, we're Yankee fans.

Burton Leiser
Briarcliff Manor, New York

It only hurts when I laugh!

Upon hearing of my recent surgery, my dear friends sadistically sent me your book, *Is God a Cubs Fan?* I had to read it with pillow over my tummy. Perhaps it could be marketed that way for the temporarily infirmed. So, as you might have surmised, this is a fan letter. It will become a keeper in my library.

Esther Blumenfeld
Tucson, Arizona

Having studied your sermons, I have concluded that the Cubs are not a Jewish team; that is your problem.

As a long time Dodger fan, I do not have this problem. Although the Dodgers have been wandering in the wilderness for many years, I am convinced that their overall (albeit periodic) success originates from originally being near the Chassidic neighborhoods of Brooklyn and the Lower East Side (where my ancestors once soujourned). The Boys of Summer are about to return to their days of glory with the arrival of Shawn Green. (Why do all Jewish kids now have Irish names)? I am sure that his mother wanted him back in Los Angeles where he could find a nice Jewish girl, although many were chasing him in Toronto. We will now return to the glory days of Sandy Koufax and Larry Sherry, neither of whom would pitch on *Yom Kippur.* This was the obvious solution for the Cubs. You missed your chance—you could have traded Samella Sosa for Shawn Green, even up.

Jay Swartz
Toronto, Ontario, Canada

I just got back from the Y—have another two chapters of Arnie's book—I'm doing the treadmill, laughing out loud. He's a great storyteller....almost makes me want to come out for services, just to hear his spiel at the end!

New York Yankees Fan

Your Cubs book is out of the park and onto Waveland Avenue! There are so many items in your book that sounded like you knew me forever!

James J. Shapiro
Largo, Florida

IS GOD A CUBS FAN?

IS GOD A CUBS FAN?

By Arnold B. Kanter

Designed & Illustrated by Darlene Grossman

Cubs Season Summaries by Sam Eifling

JRC Press • *Evanston, IL*

Illustrations © 2009 by Darlene Grossman

Is God a Cubs Fan? published 1999
Is God Still A Cubs Fan? published 2002
JRC Press, 303 Dodge Avenue, Evanston, IL 60202-3252
847.328.7678
fax 847.328.2298

Printed in the United States of America

ISBN: 0-967-64155-1

The cost of the first printing of this book was partially underwritten by an anonymous donor in memory of her dear father, who was an avid Cubs fan and a *mensch.*

The cost of this printing was underwritten by Jonathan Markowitz and Ruth Wenger, dedicated in memory of Lenore Markowitz, a lover of books, and Jonathan's beloved mother and the grandmother of Ariell and Ben.

To everyone who has kept faith, hope, and
a sense of humor in the face of all odds.

And to my father, Alexander J. Kanter, who,
despite having lived almost 93 years,
never saw the Cubs win a World Series.

Dedicated in memory of
Lenore Markowitz
Beloved mother of Jonathan (Ruth Wenger) Markowitz,
Grandmother of Ariell and Ben

CONTENTS

FOREWORD

When you write a book called *Is God a Cubs Fan?* who do you
ask to write the foreword?

Your rabbi, of course. (Presuming that is, that Ernie Banks
is unavailable). So speaking in that capacity, dear reader, it
gives me great pleasure to present this remarkable book to
you. I say this because it is filled from cover to cover with
wit, wisdom, and heart—and you don't have to be Jewish
or a baseball fan in order to enjoy it.

Is God a Cubs fan? Read on and I promise: you will
eventually learn the answer to this important theological
conundrum. Along the way you will learn a deeper truth as
well: that baseball has a *neshamah*—that is to say, a uniquely
Jewish soul.

But perhaps you are skeptical. If so, you should know that
a growing number of experts are discovering a powerful
symmetry between these two great spiritual traditions:

- Both baseball and Judaism are concerned with the
  mythic archetypes of exile and return. The ultimate goal
  of both traditions is homecoming. In baseball, players
  leave the safety of their dugout and run the base paths,

with the hope of somehow finding the way to home plate. Likewise, since the destruction of the ancient Temple, the Jewish religion has been a veritable textbook for maneuvering through the perils of exile, guided by the dream of finally returning home.

- There are no fans anywhere who are as long-suffering as baseball fans. The plaintive cry coined by Brooklyn Dodger fans, "Wait till next year!" is most certainly a derivative of "Next year in Jerusalem!"—the refrain that ends every Passover Seder.

- Just as baseball is a uniquely Jewish sport, certain baseball teams are clearly more Jewish than others. The perennially tragic fates of teams such as the Boston Red Sox, the Brooklyn Dodgers and, of course, the Chicago Cubs have had an all-too-familiar resonance for Jewish baseball fans everywhere.

As I said earlier, however, you don't have to be Jewish to appreciate these truths. They are truly universal. Arnie Kanter's words will ring true for anyone who has ever poised on the edge of a dream, only to fall off.

Indeed, you will find that Arnie Kanter is the consummate tour guide for a journey into the glorious heartbreak that is Cubs baseball. Arnie is a native Chicagoan and has suffered through countless losing seasons at Wrigley Field with a uniquely "Cubs-esque" combination of hope, fatalism, heartbreak, and utter disgust. Most important, he has a pretty deep *neshamah* himself. And I should know. I'm his rabbi.

But enough about me. It's time to play ball!

—*Rabbi Brant Rosen*

INTRODUCTION

· ·

I was born a Cubs fan, and a Jew. Not necessarily in that order. When the Cubs last played in the World Series, I was two. I don't remember much about that, but I'm told they lost to the Detroit Tigers in seven. That I can believe. My father, who died at almost 93 in 2008, was minus eight years old when the Cubs last won the World Series. He told me that he didn't remember much about it.

For better or worse—mainly worse—I remember a whole lot about the Cubs, after the age of, say, five. Alas, the Cubs occupied a large part of my life. As a child, I recall my summertime mood depending largely upon whether the Cubs had won or lost that day. I had a pretty unhappy childhood.

I'm not going to try to relive all of the ups and downs— and downs, and downs—of being a Cubs fan these past 60 years. It's too painful. Most of those moments I regret I had to live through once.

As most of us do, I've mellowed, perhaps even matured a bit, as I've waxed senior. For some reason, though, that process seems to have affected my relationship with the Cubs little, if at all. In a world increasingly devoid of guideposts, the Cubs have remained my North Star. Talk about lost. . . .

Increasingly, though, I've come to see connections between my North Star and my Jewish star. This connection is not something I set forth to find. It just happened. Slowly.

In 1983, I joined a Reconstructionist congregation. For those (many) who are not familiar with Reconstructionism, I'm sorry. But I certainly won't pretend to describe it in this book. For our purposes, it's probably sufficient to say that it is a branch of Judaism, dating back to 1922, that attempts to reconstruct the Jewish religion in a way that makes it speak more directly to modern Jews.

In Reconstructionism, tradition is important, but not controlling; it has a vote, but not a veto, in matters of observance. Reconstructionists sometimes create their own traditions or rituals, often borrowing heavily from the past. Reconstructionism tends to be inclusive and non-judgmental. It rejects the notion that the Jewish people have been chosen by God. For me, Reconstructionism has provided meaning for many things that I used to do by rote.

The Jewish Reconstructionist Congregation (JRC) of Evanston, Illinois, of which I am a card-carrying member, has many traditions (we call them *minhagim*). One is an Open Mike during the afternoon of *Yom Kippur*. At the conclusion of the morning service on this holiest of Jewish holidays, members of the congregation are invited up to the *bimah* to speak for a couple minutes on anything of importance to them.

Most of these talks are serious reflections on important people, experiences, or causes in congregants' lives, listened to empathetically by the more than one hundred people who choose to remain at the *shul* (which, by the way, is a

Methodist church rented by the congregation for the High Holidays, since the JRC synagogue building—purchased after years of heated congregational debate—was too small from the moment it was purchased to house the congregation for High Holiday services).

On *Yom Kippur,* 1984, without a great deal of planning or forethought, I found myself up on the *bimah,* reflecting on the existence of God, and discovering my answer in the Chicago Cubs. So enthusiastic was the reception to that talk, that I pursued it further the next *Yom Kippur*—and thus was a *minhag* born.

Each year I ponder the relationship between God and the Cubs, posing weighty questions that theologians have long wrestled with. For the past 25 years, my talk has been the last one given at our Open Mike, placed there, I am told, because of the reluctance of others to follow what they may consider my off-the-wall remarks and because of a sense that anticipation of these remarks serves to hold the audience. I'm often asked for copies of these talks, and have been encouraged by congregants to publish them. This book is the fruit of that encouragement.

I'm not entirely new to this business. I've written five satirical books on the law, a profession that I practiced for some 15 years. These books were occasioned originally by a need to maintain my sanity in the face of seemingly insane, sometimes almost surrealistic, experiences that I encountered, first as an associate and then as a partner at a large and prestigious law firm, and, later, as a consultant to large law firms. Though I may not always have recognized it, these writings were born of love and of a need to understand. So, too, are the writings in this book.

I hope (and pray) that these pieces may rekindle in some readers moments in their lives when they have loved, or wondered, or just plain shaken their heads. And that, for others, this book may help them to understand those seemingly incomprehensible folk—whether they be fans of the Cubs or the Dodgers, of baseball or cricket, adherents of Judaism or Buddhism—whose passion for sport or religion, or both, may seem just a bit beyond the pale.

Each of the 25 Open Mike talks is reprinted here pretty much as it was given, preceded by summaries of the sports year written—tongue planted firmly in cheek—by Sam Eifling, a journalist friend, and accompanied by explanatory notes about the season or the congregation necessary for the general reader to appreciate what was said. The design of the book and the illustrations were done lovingly by JRC member Darlene Grossman, and the entire project was shepherded through by the gentle staff of another JRC member, Dale Good, who, I note with great sadness, passed away between the original book and this printing. He is greatly missed at JRC. Finally, JRC members Adrienne Lieberman lovingly proofread the manuscript and Jeff Winter made this book accessible to those who don't speak Hebrew by providing a glossary.

In yore days, at the conclusion of the Passover *seder*, people said to one another, *"L'shana ha ba-a biyerushalayim,* next year may we meet in Jerusalem." To my friends, I wish, *"l'shana ha ba-a b'*Wrigley Field." And may the Cubs win the World Series again, come the next millennium.

1984

Pennant Fever

By most Cubs' standards, 1984 was a downright magnificent year. They established a new home attendance record by drawing more than 2 million fans, they finished the season atop their division (with a 96–65 record), won the most games since capturing 98 in 1945, and were actually favored to go to the Fall Classic. To top it off, the team they edged by 6½ games to win their division was the New York Mets, who beat out the Cubs for a playoff spot in the dregs of the 1969 season.

Individually, Rick Sutcliffe's 16–1 record earned him just the third Cy Young Award in the club's history. Second baseman Ryne Sandberg was the first Cub MVP since Mr. Cub himself, Ernie Banks, took two in a row in the late 50s. Skipper Jim Frey was named Manager of the Year. So why the long faces?

After winning their division, the Cubs whipped the San Diego Padres 13–0 and 4–2 in the first two games of the best-of-five National League Championship Series in Chicago, then proceeded to drop three straight on the West Coast. James Thompson, then Governor of Illinois, summed it up for many when he said "I feel like there's been a death in the family."

This was to be the fans' and players' absolution for a half century of going nowhere. "My ship has come in," said Ernie Banks before the National League Championship Series. "Good things come to those who wait . . . and wait . . . and wait."

So what do you say when you flip the wait light back on? "Nobody died here," Cubs outfielder Gary Matthews said. "We'll bounce back."

From success?

● ●

Does God Exist?

'D LIKE TO TAKE A MINUTE to talk to you about God. Not in the manner of a born-again Christian because, personally, I think one birth's plenty. Do you remember how dark and wet it was in there, and then they give you this narrow little channel to scrunch yourself through? *Oy,* what a trauma birth was; I'm still recovering. But I digress.

As a youth, I first puzzled about God in Hebrew school at Rodfei Zedek, a conservative synagogue on the south side of Chicago, where other JRC luminaries such as Roger Price, Alan Gratch, and the Brothers Rubin (Neal and Alan), also puzzled. At least we puzzled on days that we weren't cutting Hebrew school to play baseball in East End Park, across the street from shul. In retrospect, I think that at Rodfei Zedek we learned God by rote. I don't mean to knock that. Rote works, at least on one level. Pleasant memories survive from those days, memories of beautiful melodies in a lovely sanctuary with a thought-provoking rabbi, memories of Sunday mornings when *bar mitzvah*-age boys and their fathers ate bagels and lox and custard-filled pastries together, then *bentched* the blessings after the meal and ran across the street to play touch football.

After Rodfei Zedek, I next encountered God-puzzling in college, at Brandeis University. Now, though, our puzzling was no longer rote. We asked whether God existed. Could we prove it? Or was God, perhaps, dead. And when we studied the Book of Job, taught by a great scholar named Nahum Glatzer, we were left to wonder whether, if God indeed existed and was still alive, this was the sort of God we'd like to go out for a beer with, anyway (though I don't recall Professor Glatzer posing the question in quite that way).

After Brandeis, I took a break from my God-puzzling to attend law school and, then, to earn a few bucks as a lawyer. You might say that I drifted pretty far away from religion for the better part of 20 years, until, last year, we joined JRC. Here I found that not only was God not rote and God's existence questioned, but now I had to come to grips with the very real and troubling possibility that, if God existed, He might be a lady.

So, anyway, this High Holidays, I decided it's time—enough is enough. I'd devote the period between *Rosh Hashanah* and *Yom Kippur* to figuring out, once and for all, whether God existed. It wouldn't be easy, I knew, but what the hell.

Well, I've got some good news for you. God exists. And at the risk of seeming too much of a nutty, messianic-type personality, I would like to predict that God will soon make

His (or Her) presence visible to us in a manner such that none of us will ever again be able to doubt God's existence. As you break the fast tonight, watch for God's presence . . . on television, manifesting Himself/Herself in the miracle of the Chicago Cubs reaching the World Series.

And one final thought, if we want to improve relations with our non-Jewish brothers and sisters, we need spread only one harmless little rumor—Ryne Sandberg[1] is Jewish.

---

[1] Cubs' star second baseman. (He is not Jewish).

1985

Back to Reality

Baseball's universe righted itself quickly after the 1984 season: the Cubs began to lose again. It took a wave of injuries to drown the reigning division champs after they sailed along winning 34 of their first 53 games. The Cubs tied a club record by losing 13 straight games on the way to mediocrity, finally anchoring fourth place in the division with just under a .500 winning percentage and sinking 23½ games behind the first-place St. Louis Cardinals.

Pitching did them in. Rick Sutcliffe finished 8–8 just a year after winning the Cy Young Award. Cub pitcher Reggie Patterson became the answer to a trivia question when Pete Rose notched his 4,191st hit off of Patterson, tying Ty Cobb's record. The one Cub pitcher, though, whose '85 record kept pace with his '84 performance was relief pitcher Lee Smith. His club-high 33 saves in '85 were all the more impressive considering how few saves were available. Of Lee Smith, Ray Sons wrote in the Chicago Sun Times, *"Lee is saved for saves, and the Cubs are beyond saving."*

There were the usual offensive bright spots for the Cubbies, provided by their only All-Star, Ryne Sandberg, who led the team with

26 home runs. (The Cubs did manage to lead the National League with 150 homers). Ryno also stole 54 bases, the highest total by a Cub since "Wild Fire" Schulte swiped 57 bags in 1906.

But you can't keep Cubs' fans down—'84's coattails extended to push a club record: 2.16 million fans through the turnstiles in '85.

* *

From the Desk of God

SOME OF YOU MAY REMEMBER last *Yom Kippur,* when I predicted that God would manifest His or Her existence by ushering the Chicago Cubs into the World Series on *Yom Kippur* night. Well, the failure of that prediction to materialize generated quite a spiritual crisis within our congregation, and more than a little ugliness towards me, personally.

Leroy Shuster[1] took the Cubs' loss as proof that God was that within each of us that strove for what was good, and that there just wasn't enough striving within the Cubs. To Rabbi Arnie, of the White House,[2] it was proof that God worked in mysterious ways. And to Henry Waller,[3] with whom I went to Camp Indianola back in the 1950s, well poor Henry took it so hard that for a month he called me at 3:30 each morning and shouted, "Why did you do it?" But the most serious result of my faulty prediction was that I was sentenced to a year on the JRC Board of Directors.

---

[1] One of the founders, and a former president, of JRC.

[2] JRC's rabbi, Arnie Rachlis, spent his sabbatical year serving as a White House Fellow in Washington, DC.

[3] JRC board member

So you'd think I'd have enough sense to keep my mouth shut this year, but noooo.

Actually, I have remained preoccupied with the existence of God. For *Chanukah* last year my daughters, Jodi and Wendy, bought me a pad of notepaper that says *From the Desk of God* at the top, with a thunderbolt through the O, and ever since, miraculously, my daughters have been receiving notes from God. They gave me permission to share the two most recent notes with you.

FROM THE DESK OF

September 24, 1985

Dear Jodes,

Many times I hear, "Why do the Jews fast on Yom Kippur?" *The short answer, of course, is "If not the Jews, who then?"*

Historically, non-Jews have rarely fasted on Yom Kippur, *unless they are unbelievably* frum. *While this could change any minute, I'm not counting on it. So it is left to the Jews to fast because I brought them out of Egypt, and for many other good reasons, as well.*

The first recorded fast was Harry Cohen, in 422, either B.C.E. *or* C.E., *they forgot to record that; but, in any case, plenty long ago. Harry did not fast the entire day. He had a little* nosh *around one and a banana at four thirty. Other than this, though, he abstained.*

The second recorded fast was in 1958—also, by coincidence, Harry Cohen (but a different one), who didn't eat all day, and died. This they don't print in the Bible.   —God

FROM THE DESK OF GOD

Dear Wendzo,

Why do we blow the ram's horn to herald the New Year, and also for Yom Kippur? Though it's true that it is very difficult to blow the ram's horn and get that shrill sound, it is even more difficult to get that sound by blowing any other part of the ram; if you've ever tried, you know.

You may remember that as Abraham was about to sacrifice his son Isaac, a ram appeared in the bush and Abraham burned the ram instead of Isaac. This may seem like a good thing to you, but the rams are not so nuts about the story. In fact, this explains why so few rams are Jewish (and also, perhaps, why so few Isaacs are rammish). Even the Los Angeles Rams football team has very few Jews on it, because most of them decided to become doctors or rabbis. Another reason is that the football is made of pig's skin, which is trayf, so many potential Hasidic superstars wouldn't touch it. Save the rams! —God

For any of you who still doubt the existence of God, even after hearing these authentic letters—well, the Chicago Bears are 3 and 0.

1986

An UnBearable Year

The Cubs' downward spiral that had begun in 1985 continued to deepen into 1986. Jim Frey, who had been Manager of the Year just two years earlier, was fired in June as the Cubs wallowed near the bottom of their division. Gene Michaels was installed, but he could hardly stop the tailspin. Chicago finished 70–90, a full 37 games behind the first-place New York Mets. Said third-base coach Don Zimmer, "I don't think God could have come down and made this team win."

For the record, second-baseman Ryne Sandberg and catcher Jody Davis tried their best to compensate for God's (and the pitching staff's) shortcomings. Both were All-Stars and Gold Glove winners. Davis' 21 home runs paced the Cubs, who led the National League in homers for the second straight year with 155. Sandberg was again spectacular on defense, setting a major-league record by committing only five errors at second base and fielding a stellar .993 for the year.

But a rash of injuries to the pitching staff proved too much for the solid hitting and defense to overcome. Rick Sutcliffe's bum *shoulder led him into a dismal 5–14 showing, after going 24–9 over the two preceding years. Unfortunately, his misery invited company as the Cubs' pitching staff lacked a 10-game winner for the first time in their 111-year history and posted the highest team ERA (4.49) in the National League. The axiom that pitching is 50 percent of baseball proved true. The club settled into a fifth-place finish in the NL Eastern Division with a winning percentage of just .438.*

The Refrigerator of Life

FOR TWO YEARS NOW, WE have wrestled with the question that our ancient rabbis and scholars have struggled with over the centuries on *Yom Kippur*. Just what is the relationship between God, the Jewish people, and sports, anyway? Actually, I've been wrestling with that question. You pretty much just sit there and listen (and I need hardly point out that wrestling is itself a sport, but not one for a Jewish boy).

Now, of course, volumes have been written on the parallels between the Cubs and the Jewish people. I mean, who can attribute to mere coincidence the fact that the Jews wandered for 40 years in the desert and the Cubs have wandered for more than 40 years through the so-called "friendly confines"[1] without winning a pennant—and without lights. And doesn't Sandberg sound sorta Jewish to you? I know it does to me.

---

[1] Wrigley Field, home of the Cubs, is often referred to as the "Friendly Confines," the description given to it by former Cub great, Ernie Banks.

But much less has been written on the parallels between the Chicago Bears and the Jewish people. Personally, I attribute this to the fact that, unlike the Jewish people, the Bears generally don't suffer much—their opponents do. This *Rosh Hashanah*, though, I began to ponder this question, prompted by something our rabbi said in his sermon. And for those of you who don't listen to our rabbi, maybe this will be a lesson to you as to what you can expect, if you do. Anyway, Arnie talked about how this Hebrew year, 5747, ends with the numbers 747 (not, in itself, a particularly astounding observation, I might add). For a horrible second I thought, oh, no, 747, he's going to call this the year of the jumbo jet and tell us more about his adventures in Washington. Instead, though, he pointed out how 7-4-7 add up to 18 (I confirmed this with my calculator) and how 18 stands for *chai* which means life.

Now what does all of this have to do with the Chicago Bears? Well, I suppose the answer is pretty obvious to most of you. Who is the Bears' popular folk hero this year? William "Refrigerator" Perry.[2] What is the Fridge's number? 72. And what is 72? Four *chai*. So I began combing the sporting goods stores all around Chicago to see whether anyone had recognized, and capitalized financially upon, this rather obvious fact. And, to my shock and dismay, I found that nobody had. So I had this sweatshirt made up. And since, besides listening to our rabbi, I also listened to our president talk on *Rosh Hashanah* about how the congregation needs funds, I'm going to suggest to our fundraising committee that we have more of these sweatshirts made up, and sell them for a mere four *chai* each.[3]

---

[2] A 300-pound-plus Bears lineman who, because of his tremendous bulk, was nicknamed "The Refrigerator."

[3] Like most of my brilliant financial ideas, this one was never implemented.

1987

Blank Check MVP

Since its opening in 1914, Wrigley Field has been known as a beautiful place to watch a baseball game—as they say, easy on the eyes. In 1987, it picked up an MVP-caliber player because it was easy on the knees, too.

After 11 years with the Montreal Expos, who play on artificial turf, outfielder Andre Dawson decided his knees needed soft grass underneath them, and practically got down on one of them asking the Cubs to sign him. Pitcher Rick Sutcliffe was so excited about the prospect of playing with Dawson that he said he'd donate $100,000 toward signing him. After numerous snubs and snags from the Cubs' front office, Dawson presented the Cubs with a signed contract with the salary amount left blank. The Cubs filled in a bargain-basement price of $500,000. Dawson was worth every cent.

Andre won a Gold Glove award, as did second baseman Ryne Sandberg, but Dawson's true calling was as a slugger. He slammed 49 home runs, the most by a Cub since Hack Wilson in 1930. He batted .296 with 137 RBIs, became only the 12th Cub to hit for the cycle[1] on April 29 and established a modern Cubs record for home

---

[1] Hit a single, double, triple and home run in one game.

runs in a month with 15 in August. (August was also the month that the Cubs retired Hall-of-Famer Billy Williams' number 26, which now flies at Wrigley Field from the flag pole in right, where he played outfield). Andre led the National League in home runs, RBIs and total bases. Fans in the right field bleachers began to greet their star, as he trotted out to his position, with a stand-and-bow routine known as "salaams."

For his remarkable year, Dawson won the MVP award—the first time the award had gone to a player on a last-place team. Rick Sutcliffe also had a banner year, winning 18 games and falling just two votes shy of the Cy Young award. Still, the team found winning difficult, finishing 76–85. After a brief fling in first place in late May, the Cubs generously let every other team in the NL East pass, handing out a team-record 628 walks along the way.

Cubs fans apparently didn't mind much, though: The '87 team became the first last-place NL team to draw over 2 million in home attendance.

• •

The Sacrificing by Isaac

FOR THE LAST THREE *Yom Kippurs* (or is it *Yoms Kippur?*), I have spoken about God and Judaism and sports. And a lot of you have laughed. And I have to tell you now that that laughter has hurt me deeply. Because those talks were not meant to be funny. I take my God seriously and I take my Judaism seriously and, most of all, I take my sports seriously. So, this year, I decided not to risk being misunderstood and, in lieu of speaking of the Cubs or the Bears (about both of which there is precious little to say, in any case), I decided to talk about the *Rosh Hashanah Torah* portion in which God instructs Abraham to take his favorite son, Isaac, up to Mount Moriah and there to bind him and offer him as a sacrifice.

Now, of course, scholars have struggled with this *parsha* for centuries. What kind of a God would ask Abraham to give up his most loved son? What kind of a man would offer up his son, even at the insistence of God? And I read many interpretations of the story, some claiming that God was merely testing Abraham, some arguing that it was Abraham testing God. And all of these interpretations are interesting, but none of them seems to me satisfactory.

So I began my own search for an explanation that would be true to the text and might, at the same time, allow me to emerge with my respect for both God and Abraham intact. This search has not been easy. It has led me back to inspect many original historical documents—the Dead Sea Scrolls, the Red Sea Scrolls, several boxes of letters in Abraham's own hand. And, at last, I believe I have found the answer.

Abraham was very old—100 years when Isaac was born. And we know Abraham was hard of hearing. This we can discern directly from the *Torah*. How? When God speaks to Abraham and tells him to take Isaac to Mount Moriah, he says, " Take your son," and, though the text does not reflect it, Abraham says, "Huh?" And, so, God continues, "your favored one" and Abraham says, "Eh?" and God finally

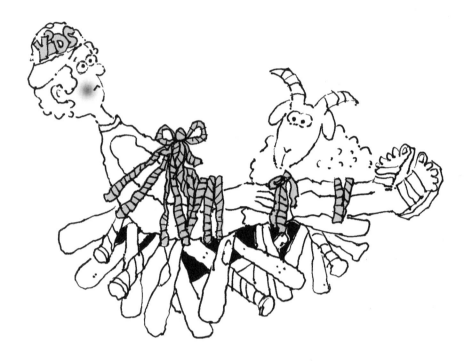

shouts, "*ISAAC!*" Later, when Abraham is about to kill Isaac, you will recall that the angel has to shout to him twice, "Abraham, Abraham," because Abraham does not hear the angel the first time.

Now we know that Isaac was not a young child when he was taken by Abraham to Moriah. And from the Red Sea Scrolls, I discovered—and this is not generally known—that Isaac was quite athletic. Indeed, he played left field for the Yisraeli *Yids*. And, just before God spoke to Abraham, it is recorded in those scrolls, the *Yids* had dropped a real heartbreaker to the Philistine Pirates, 5–4, when Isaac grounded into a game-ending triple play, with men on first and second and nobody out. This loss dropped the *Yids* into a tie for second place.

Now the Lord was plenty ticked off at Abraham, Isaac's coach, when this happened, and He spoke to Abraham saying, not, as the Bible says, "Take your son, your favored one, Isaac, whom you love, and go to the land of Moriah, and offer him there as a sacrifice on one of the heights which I will point out to you," but rather, "When you take your son, your favored son, Isaac, whom you love and go to the field of the first place Moriah Mountaineers, tell him there to sacrifice, when I point it out to you." So, in the *Akedah,* God is not testing Abraham at all, but reprimanding him for his lousy baseball strategy. And the real pathos in the story is that old Abraham's defective hearing almost turned a sacrifice bunt into a sacrifice of his son, thus converting the bunting of Isaac into the binding of Isaac. Out of this near tragic episode, the rabbis tell us, came the use of hand signals to batters.

1988

All-Stars in the Dark

*Sandwiched between Andre Dawson's incredible 1987 season and
the miraculous 1989 season was a pedestrian fourth-place Cubs
finish in 1988. The most historically significant of the 77 wins that
year came on August 9, when the Cubs beat the New York Mets
6–4. Defeating the Mets is always cause for celebration, but this
particular victory came in the first night game ever played at
Wrigley Field. For the first time in the 74-year history of Wrigley, no
one had to skip school or work to go root for the Cubs on a Monday.*

*A more dubious Wrigley tradition persisted, however—the Cubs
produced some outstanding individual performances en route to
losing more than half their games. Pitcher Greg Maddux blossomed
early in the season and finished 18–8. At 22, the right-hander
became the youngest ever Cub All-Star, and the first Cub since
1971 to defeat every team in the league at least once. No other Cub
starter finished above .500 for the year, though Rick Sutcliffe did
manage to steal home on July 29.*

*Coming off his MVP year, Andre Dawson again led the team
in home runs (24) and RBIs (79). He hit .303, earned his 8th*

Gold Glove award, and set a major league record with his twelfth
straight season with at least 10 home runs and 10 stolen bases.
Ryne Sandberg added to his growing legend by whapping his 100th
career home run. First baseman Mark Grace was named Sporting
News *NL Rookie of the Year after hitting .296—the best for a Cubs*
rookie in 15 years. Oddly enough, all seven of his home runs that
year were on the road.

But even with six All-Stars on the roster, the Cubs finished a
dismal 24 games back of the first-place Dodgers. Manager Don
Zimmer didn't see much reason to expect better than a .500 finish
in 1989. Zim was known for his keen baseball instincts, but as it
turned out, he dropped the ball on that prognostication.

● ●

Does God Want Lights in Wrigley Field?

ET ME BE HONEST. I was going to skip the *Open Mike* this
year. But the demand was so overwhelming—not one,
but two people asked me whether I was going to
speak—that, in the end, I've relented.

In past years, I've touched not only on God, but sports.
This year, the natural choice would have been to turn to the
Olympics. But when I heard the groans that greeted Rabbi
Arnie on *erev Rosh Hashanah* when he referred to the High
holidays as our s-o-u-l Olympics,[1] I quickly canned that idea.
Thanks a lot, Rabbi.

By the way, I almost missed *erev Rosh Hashanah* altogether,

---

[1] The 1988 Olympics were held in Seoul, South Korea.

because of the finals of the U.S. Open tennis tournament. For those of you of Orthodox background, who felt compelled to leave early to get to services on time, Mats Willanderstein beat Ivan Lendlberg in five sets.[2] Tennis, of course, is a great Jewish game. Though it is not generally known, tennis was invented by a group of rabbis. How do I know this? Easy. You think maybe a bunch of *goyim* would have come up with a scoring system that goes—love, fifteen, thirty and forty, with six games to a set, and foot faults?

But enough frivolity. I want to try to put to rest, once and for all, the question that Chicago rabbis have struggled with all year—does God want lights in Wrigley Field? In seeking to answer this question, I turned first to the text of the *Torah*. There, I was surprised to find remarkably little on point. I know that some would point to the opening verses of Genesis, in which, as many of you may recall, God created light and saw that it was good. But, according to Rashi,[3] this passage refers to daylight, not to ballpark lights. Rashi concluded, therefore, that God did not want night games.

Moses Maimonides[4] (whose views, in my opinion, are afforded far too much weight just because of his first name) came to exactly the opposite view. Oddly enough, the views of another Moses, Moses Malone[5], are afforded only about

---

[2] Mats Willander beat Ivan Lendl in a match that ended just as services were scheduled to begin.

[3] Great commentator on the Torah, not to be confused with Vic Rashi, pitcher for the New York Yankees in the 1950s.

[4] Another famous scholar and commentator.

[5] A very large professional basketball player.

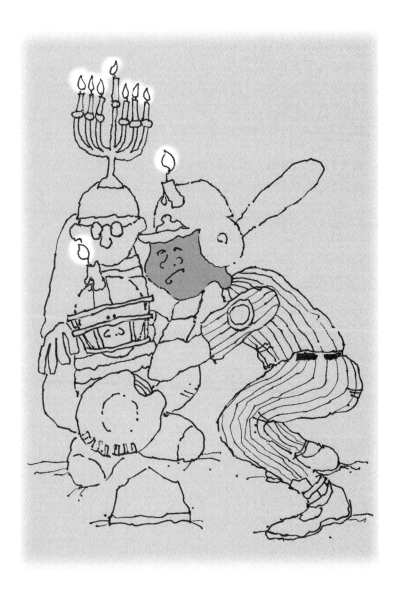

average weight, unless he looks like he might be inclined to
fight about them, in which case they are afforded a healthy
deference. (Malone, however, is paid a lot more than Maimonides ever was. Maimonides was an excellent point guard,
but suffered greatly in his compensation because all of his

team's games happened to be on Friday night and Saturday, and he was *shomer shabbos*). So far as I know, Moses Malone has never expressed an opinion as to whether God wanted lights in Wrigley Field.

Speaking of Moses, most of you recall when the Red Sea parted. I don't mean that you actually recall it, but you've probably read about it. Often, when I read the *Torah*, I long for the good old days of miracles and signs from the Lord— rods turning into serpents, frogs, locusts—those sorts of things. And every once in awhile, those signs still appear. In this driest and hottest of all summers, where drought struck the entire country, can anyone really believe that it was a coincidence that the Cubs first scheduled night game was rained out?

Sometimes God's meanings aren't all that mysterious.

1989

Pennant Fever Again

The forecast for 1989 called for another drought when the Cubs went an ignominious 9–23 in spring exhibition games. But when they started playing for keeps, the outlook changed. The Cubs held first place for 25 straight days in May and June, and were only a game and a half behind the Montreal Expos at the All-Star break.

Credit the mercurial performances of first-years Dwight Smith, Lloyd McClendon, and Jerome Walton for the Cubs' sudden fortunes. Credit Manager Don Zimmer's brash, savvy play calling that earned him Manager of the Year honors. Credit improved pitching from Greg Maddux and Rick Sutcliffe. Credit 36 saves by acquisition Mitch "Wild Thing" Williams. Credit the Cubbies. They skipped their traditional early September swoon and clinched the division by the 26th, finishing 93–69, six games in front of the New York Mets.

For the first time ever, the Cubs finished with the highest batting average in the National League two years in a row. Ryne Sandberg hit 30 home runs, the most by a Cubs second baseman in 70 years and set a record by playing 90 consecutive errorless games after June 20. Jerome Walton won the National League Rookie of the Year award, the first Cub since 1962 to do so. If that weren't proof enough of the Cubs young talent, Dwight Smith finished second in the voting.

The Cubs faced the San Francisco Giants in the Championship Series. In 1908, your ancestors might recall, the Cubs beat the Giants, who at that time hailed from Brooklyn, on the Cubs' way to their last World Series title of the century. Would the Cubs atone for their 1984 meltdown against the Padres?

Sophomore first baseman Mark Grace did his best to pull the Cubs into the Fall Classic with his 11 hits for 17 at bats, 8-RBI performance in the five game series. However, his Giant counter-part, Will Clark, set major league records with 13 hits, 8 runs, and a mammoth .650 batting average in leading the Giants to a 4–1 series win. The sun sets in the West, after all, and the Cubs' surprising flood of success finally evaporated.

The team that spent so much of the season in first place also had, as usual, first-rate fans. Almost 2.5 million of them swept through Wrigley Field turnstiles, the most in 114 years of Cubs baseball. When the Cubs reign, fans pour in.

An earthquake struck San Francisco during the World Series, postponing several games. Alas, no quake struck Chicago.

• •

Is Baseball Anti-Semitic?

I'M NOT HAPPY TO BE HERE. For me, Open Mike evokes some of the worst moments of my life.

In 1984, my first Open Mike, I predicted that God would prove His existence as He sent the Cubs into the World Series by beating the San Diego Padres. You all know what happened. And many members of this congregation have not forgotten yet. Each year, when I hear the rabbi say how everyone should forgive everyone else for the sins they may have inadvertently committed, I think, "Aha, this year they're going to flock up to me and say, 'Arnie, we forgive you, we know you didn't do that on purpose.'" But has even one person come up to say that to me—*hell no.*

Some of you may have expected me to moan and groan about the Cubs being down three games to one in the playoffs, just taking the field for the fifth game as we sit here. But that doesn't bother me. It's just not their turn yet. Geez, they won it all in 1908, do you expect them to do it *every* year?

No, what bothers me is that this year I have been forced to confront, head-on, a very painful fact, the fact that the sport I love most, baseball, is anti-Semitic. To be honest, I've suspected it for some time. But, until this year, I've swept it under the rug.

Why did I suspect it? Little things. They add a team in San Diego and what do they call them—the San Diego *Padres.* And the St Louis Cardinals? Sure, they have a *bird* on the uniform, but they don't fool this Jew. Have you heard of the New York Rabbis or the Philadelphia *Chazans*? No, neither have I. And you go out to the game and try to get something to eat. Do they serve *knishes*? *Gefilte* fish? No, hot dogs, *trayf.*

So I suspected it. But, this year, they prove it. What do they do? Schedule Cubs playoff games on both *erev Yom Kippur* and *Yom Kippur* afternoon. When I pointed out this clear anti-Semitism to a friend, he said I was overreacting.

"First of all," he said, "the Cubs don't have any Jewish

players, so it won't affect them."

"Well, that's what a lot of people think," I said. "But it's not true; they do have a Jewish player, a starter, he just changed his name so that people don't know it."

Well, my friend perked up at this. "Who is it?" he asked.

"Promise not to tell anyone," I said, "because this guy really doesn't want it to be known."

"I promise," my friend said.

"Okay, *Shayna* Dunstein,[1] the shortstop."

"Noooo," my friend said in disbelief. "But even so, that doesn't prove anti-Semitism, he protested. Not only Jews are Cubs fans," he said.

Well, I've decided to test that out. How many of you here today are Cubs fans, raise your hand. Okay, now how many of you are Jewish?

Uh-huh, just what I thought.

Anyway, all of this raises the ethical question, can we watch the Cubs on *Yom Kippur?* Frankly, I was shocked and dismayed that there are not television monitors positioned around the sanctuary during the service. Seriously. I figure that if we can have a video camera on *Rosh Hashanah* to attract a couple of Lutheran German clergy, we sure as hell can have some TVs on *Yom Kippur* to attract several hundred Chicago-area Jews.[2]

---

[1] Really, Shawon Dunston

[2] In a controversial decision, the rabbi allowed a local TV station to film the Lutheran bishop of Berlin and his entourage, who came as guests of the congregation during *Rosh Hashanah* services.

But, we've got to face reality. Look around. There are no TVs.

So, what to do—go home to watch the game or stay at services? Well, I think that this one is really between each person and his or her God. But, I can tell you what I'm going to do after Open Mike—go to a study group here, and I'll tell you why. I like to avoid ethical questions whenever possible, and this one's easy. One of two things is going to happen this afternoon. Either the Cubs will win, and then I'll be able to see them play game six on Wednesday. Or they lose—and, I ask you, do I need the aggravation of watching them do that, on an empty stomach, yet?

So, today I'll be *frum*. Now if this were the seventh game, *oy*, would I have something to repent for next year.

1990

Going Fourth Once More

*In 1985, coming off a division title, the Cubs finished 77–84, in
fourth place. In 1990, again coming off a division title, the Cubs
finished 77–85, in fourth place.*

*The Cubs had history on their side. In 1945, the year they last
went to a World Series, the Cubs finished in first place, 89-63. Two
years after that, the Cubs were 69–85, in sixth place. Of course, it
used to be harder to manage 85 losses, back when the seasons were
154 games. But the Cubs were equal to the task.*

*Even the burden of history couldn't account for the team's 1990
plummet, though; the cast was almost identical to 1989's, indicat-
ing that the previous year, as many had suspected, was a fluke. You
can hardly blame skipper Don Zimmer for trying to lighten the
clubhouse mood occasionally. The grizzled old cherub was capable
of almost anything, both on and off the field.*

*On July 18, when Greg Maddux hadn't won in 13 starts,
Zimmer announced that he'd swim Lake Michigan if his star right-
hander beat the Padres that day. Maddux went out and won 4–2.
After being inundated with flippers and goggles, Zimmer, laugh-
ingly, admitted that he didn't even know how to swim.*

In the final game of the season, the Cubs faced the Philadelphia Phillies with only fourth place at stake. Hearing that outfielder Andre Dawson had joked that he was going to manage that night's game, Zimmer said, "Tell him he can manage." Dawson, who led the club with a .310 average and 104 RBIs that year, finished the season 1–0 as a manager. Maddux threw eight innings and batted in a crucial run when Dawson gave him the hit sign on a 2–0 count in the fifth.

Sure, Dawson could manage. The question has always been, can the Cubs?

Reconstructing the Season

I T'S GOOD TO BE BACK UP at the pulpit at our little *shul-away-from-shul*.[1] I was happy to hear Arnie say on *Rosh Hashanah* that the pastor of this *shul* is going to visit our *shul*. I'm planning to come when he does. Not because I'm that interested in what he has to say. But I can't wait to see whether they cover up our ark and *shlep* over a cross.[2]

But I digress. Once again, I find myself under enormous pressure. You may think this melodramatic or lacking in humility, but, from talking to you all on *Rosh Hashanah*, it seems to me that about 70 percent of the attendance on *Yom Kippur* is attributable to baseball *midrashim* rather than atone-

---

[1] In 1989, services were held at a local school. In 1990, they returned to our regular spot—First United Methodist Church.

[2] Each year the congregation moves a portable ark that holds the Torah over to the church, and we cover up the prominent carvings of Jesus and saints behind the altar.

ment. Now, I would never actually say that, because I know it would hurt Rabbi Arnie deeply—and then I'd know that I was one of those people he forgives from the pulpit each year.[3] But if, perchance, he overhears this, I want to ask his forgiveness, even if what I say is perfectly true—which we all know it is.

But what to talk about? The perennial problem. I suppose I could turn to optimistic topics, like the Bears being 3–0. Or the Bulls' prospects for this year. Or I could wax nostalgic, about the White Sox's last year of playing in Comiskey Park, and all the happy memories from there. But, let's be honest, how many of you are breaking the fast at Comiskey Park for the last night game there?

But *Yom Kippur* is not a time for optimism and nostalgia. No. It's a time for wallowing in misery. So I must revert to the primary source of real misery for all Jews—the Chicago Cubs. Oh, I know there are problems in the world that some might consider more serious—anti-Semitism, Saddam Hussein, homelessness. Yes, those are serious, too. But, somehow, the Cubs' predicament seems quintessentially Jewish. Particularly so because I've always had the nagging feeling that we Jews should be able to do something to solve it. Until recently, though, the answer had eluded me. This year, I figured it out. What the Cubs need is a Reconstructionist approach to baseball.

Look, follow me, here's what we do. First, we get Arnie selected commissioner of baseball. Hell, if he can be elected

---

[3] Rabbi Arnie Rachlis used to publicly ask forgiveness from the *bimah* from anyone he might have offended in the prior year.

president of the Chicago Board of Rabbis,[4] getting him named commissioner ought to be a piece of *challah*. If necessary, we organize. We ask, "just how long has it been since we've had a Jewish commissioner?" We strike—we refuse to eat hot dogs (do you really believe the kosher hot dogs at the ballpark are kosher?). If necessary, we stay away from games altogether.

So they elect Arnie. "What then?" you ask. I'll tell you what then, if you'll just be a little patient. Baseball ends around *Yom Kippur*, right? And the Cubs are rarely in first place then. But, as Reconstructionist Jews, who decides when *Yom Kippur* comes—damn right, Rabbi Arnie. I'll be looking for *Yom Kippur* around May 15 next year, when the Cubs are in first. Then we do the same thing with the playoffs and the World Series: they end when Rabbi Arnie says they end—and if that just happens to be when the Cubs are leading, well so be it.

"But is this fair?" you ask. "Does it give each team an equal chance?" Don't talk to me about equality, talk to me about justice. How many of you can still see the ground ball going through Leon Durham's legs in 1984? Every night I see it.

There are other benefits to this approach. Think of what it will do for the Reconstructionist movement in general, and for membership in JRC. Of course, this growth will create some problems. We will no longer be able to hold High Holiday Services in this church/shul—it will be much too small. Fortunately, with Arnie as commissioner, the solution is clear—*l'shana ha ba-a b'*Wrigley Field.

---

[4] Incredibly, Arnie, as a Reconstructionist, was elected president of the Board, which is dominated by more traditional rabbis.

1991

Paying for Mediocrity

Baseball teams can be like gifts to your mom: Spending more doesn't necessarily make them better. A case in point would be the 1991 Cubs, who increased their payroll by more than 90 percent over the 1990 club, but won the same number of games, 77, and again finished fourth.

The Cubs were mathematically eliminated from playoff contention on September 18. They beat the New York Mets that day, but the Pittsburgh Pirates also won, solidifying their claim to the division crown. The Chicago Tribune *headline the next morning summed it up well: "Maddux shines, but Cubs still eliminated." Greg Maddux picked up his 12th victory (to go with 10 losses), but was understandably subdued afterwards. "I felt like I've let some games slip away this year," he said. "That's behind me now. I remember those games, but I don't worry about them. There's nothing I can do about it now."*

Maddux need not have hung his head, though. He was the only pitcher to throw even one shutout for the Cubs (he threw two) and led the staff in wins (15), starts (37), innings pitched (263), strike-

outs (198), and offensive runs scored (8). The only other starter with as many as 10 wins was Mike Bielecki, who finished 13–11 with an ERA of 4.50. Southpaw reliever Chuck McElroy set a club rookie record for appearances (71) on his way to six wins, three saves, and a 1.95 ERA.

But if you're the finger-pointing type, you must look at the batting lineup first. The only Cub to hit above .300 for the year was substitute Doug Strange, who in three games went 4-for-9 at the plate. Among regulars, Ryne Sandberg's .291 led a team that hit an aggregate .253. Andre Dawson's 31 home runs accounted for about a fifth of the team's league-leading total of 159, but he hit for only a .272 average.

Manager Don Zimmer was canned on May 20. Joe Altobelli managed the 38th game of the season, an 8–6 loss to the Mets, and was subsequently succeeded by Jim Essian, who was fired on October 19.

Meanwhile, in another part of the city, the Chicago Bulls won their first NBA championship. The franchise had been around since the 1966/67 season, so it took them a while. But Chicago sport fans know about patience.

● ●

Converting the Heathen

LET ME BE HONEST—IT'S NICE to be the only Arnie up on the bimah.[1]

I don't want to give you the wrong impression. Arnie has had a very profound influence on my life. Many of you

---

[1] Rabbi Arnie Rachlis was on sabbatical.

may be unaware that, when I joined this congregation, my name was Chayim Kanter.

It's not just Arnie's name that's influenced me, though, but his actions as well. Right now, for example, Arnie's in Southern California, spreading the gospel-according-to-Kaplan,[2] trying to tilt wayward Jews towards Reconstructionism. I may be way off here, but I envision him leading a sort of modern-day crusade of Volvos and BMWs down the freeways of Los Angeles, seeking to convert the heathen.

Don't get me wrong, I think that's very important work. Like the rest of you, I've been shocked and dismayed to read the articles about how many Jews we're losing, through intermarriage and otherwise. Personally, though, I think we should be taking a far more aggressive approach to this problem than Arnie is. It's fine to try to bring drifting Jews home to Judaism, but why not go after that huge market of people who have never experienced the joys of *Yiddish*? That's where the real opportunity lies.

So I asked myself, what's keeping more people from converting to Judaism? I pondered this during last Saturday night's Cubs-Expos game (which, with an incredible comeback from a 5–0 deficit, the Cubs won 7–5 in ten innings). Of course, as a sensitive human being, I felt great joy after that game. But I wondered why I did not feel fulfillment as a Jew, why I didn't feel *nachas*. The answer became clear to me on the El trip home: the entire experience was *goyish*. Indeed,

---

[2] Mordecai Kaplan, the founder of Reconstructionism.

glancing down at my scorecard, I noticed that not a single Cubs player is Jewish. Now that fact might not cause those of us who have endured the pain of circumcision and the trauma of *bar mitzvah* to leave the faith. But who the hell would want to convert to a religion that not a single Cub player would choose? Not me, that's for sure. So I've hatched a plan to make attending Wrigley Field a more Jewish experience next season. Here are the steps I've taken so far:

1. The team name has been changed to the Chicago *Cubbelas*.

2. Next year, when a home run is hit, you'll hear Harry Caray shout, "There's a long drive, it might be, it could be, it is a home run, *VAY IZ MIR!*"[3]

3. During the first rain delay next year, Steve Stone is going to reveal that Andre Dawson has agreed to change his name back to his original—*Avram Dawstein*.

4. Vendors will sell gefilte fish with little packets of red and white horseradish; and *Mogen David* wine instead of *Budweiser*—but not after the seventh inning.

5. Before turning the lights on for night games Wayne Messmer will recite a *bracha* ending with "*l'hadlik ner shel Cubbelas.*"[4]

6. The name "Bleacher Bums" has been changed to "Bleacher *Bochers*."

---

[3] Caray used to end his home run calls with "HO–LY COW!"

[4] Messmer sings the "Star Spangled Banner" at Cubs home games. The suggestion is that he switch to a blessing over the lights.

7. On June 16, the first 5,000 fans to enter the park will receive *mezzuzot*.

8. After each *Cubbela* victory, the fans will put their arms around each other and chant *shehehianu*.[5]

9. And, finally, we have bought advertising time and I'm proud to announce that Reconstructionism has been named the official religion of the Chicago *Cubbelas*.

This plan is not going to be cheap. But the future of American Jewry may well hinge on its success. So I appeal to you all to contribute as generously as you can to the new American Jewry/Chicago *Cubbela* fund that's been established at JRC. Next year, we'll not just get excited about a *Cubbela* victory—we'll *kvell*. *L'shana haba-a b'*Wrigley Field.

---

[5] A traditional prayer of thanks, sung in JRC with people putting their arms around one another.

1992

Say Goodbye to Cy

Despite the amazing year pitcher Greg Maddux had in 1992—National League Cy Young Award, Gold Glove Award, All-Star starter, 20–11 record, tied for the league lead in victories, third-lowest ERA (2.18)—he will be remembered best by Cubs fans for what he didn't do: re-sign with the Cubs.

After the best year by a Cubs pitcher since Rick Sutcliffe in 1984, Maddux went to the Atlanta Braves as a free agent, signing for $28 million over five years, just $500,000 more than the Cubs had offered. In Atlanta, he won the next three Cy Young Awards. New Cubs general manager Larry Hines had been lax in renewing Maddux's contract, and Maddux, probably the pitcher of the decade for the 1990s, had other options.

Maddux went on to win a World Series with the Braves while the Cubs . . . well, the Cubs were consistently the Cubs. They finished in fourth place in 1992 for the third straight year, and at 78–84, had just one more win than they'd had in either of the previous two years. In the eight years since going to the National League Championship Series in 1984, the club had won 76, 77, or 78 games six times.

It wasn't as though the club didn't play well—it was more that they didn't play well until they had settled at the bottom of the division. The Cubs hadn't won 18 games in a month since July 1989, but they won 18 in both June and August. They set defensive marks for most errorless games in a season (88) and highest fielding percentage (.982). And Hines finagled a trade that sent unhappy slugger George Bell to the White Sox in exchange for future MVP Sammy Sosa.

The other Cubs All-Star besides Maddux was stalwart Ryne Sandberg, who made his ninth appearance at the midsummer classic. He led NL second basemen in assists (539) for the seventh time and didn't commit a throwing error for the second consecutive season. He also hit 26 home runs and batted .304. Appropriately, Sandberg became the game's highest-paid player when the Cubs awarded him a four-year, $30.5 million extension in spring training.

Were it not for a baldheaded icon playing basketball on the South Side, Sandberg might have been Chicago's most beloved athlete. But since the Michael Jordan–led Chicago Bulls won their second-straight NBA title, Sandberg couldn't even claim to be the city's favorite number 23.

Sin in the Bleachers

OY, WHAT TO TALK ABOUT this year? I've had a lot of suggestions. Many people have come up and asked why I always have to talk about the Cubs. *Yom Kippur* is depressing enough. Why not talk about the Bulls this year, they ask. And I must admit, that is

tempting. After all, the Bulls are a Chicago team. And they have won two world championships in a row. So why not talk about the Bulls?

I'll tell you why not. I ask you, is professional basketball a Jewish sport? Can a Jewish guy really relate to ten Goliaths racing up and down the court at about a zillion miles an hour when his people took 40 years to cross a damn desert? That's right, 40 years. And you know how far they actually went, I mean if they'd gone in a straight line—less than 250 miles. That's 6 miles a year, or 29 yards a day, or, if you figure an eight-hour work day, less than 4 yards an hour. At that rate, it would take $3\frac{1}{2}$ days to get from here to the Davis Street Fishmarket.[1] If this is the pace at which your ancestors traveled, are you going to enjoy professional basketball? I don't think so.

Another thing about basketball: it's anti-Semitic. Did you ever notice all those guys who, before they shoot a free throw, cross themselves? But did you ever see anybody *davenning* at the free throw line? I mean they've got enough for a *minyan*, there are ten of them out there. But do they *daven*? No.

And another thing, they call it the free throw line, or the charity line, but do you ever hear them call it the *tzedakah* line? Hell, no.

And do you see any Jewish guys on the Bulls? No. And you're not likely to, either. Just try to imagine the Bulls announcer at the stadium—the lights go out and spotlights

---

[1] A restaurant located a block from the church where JRC High Holiday services are held.

swirl all around as he calls out, "and in the middle, wearing number eighteen, *chai*, from Yeshiva University, Kareem-Abdul Goldstein."

No, basketball is not a game you talk about on *Yom Kippur*. Baseball is a game you talk about on *Yom Kippur*. But what to say? For the last two and a half weeks I have been in something of a dither. Just 17 days ago today the Cubs were mathematically eliminated from this year's division race. Of course a big surprise to me is something this did not come as. Then why should it bother me? (Not that it bothers me that much. I mean I'm functioning—sort of. Well it has been only 17 days. It's not like I've had months to get over this.)

I have to be honest, though. At times I have despaired. Just the other day, in a weak moment, I said to my wife, "Why couldn't I have been born in Oakland?" But it is not the tradition of Jews to despair. (Okay, it is, but we're trying to break out of it). In my more religious moods I feel confident that all of this is part of a plan that God has for Cubs fans. Not a very good plan, perhaps, but a plan. So the question becomes, just what is God's plan for the Cubs? Why, with the talent they've had for the last three years, have they not won a pennant? Have we Cubs fans committed some grievous sin that has prevented that? Unfortunately, I'm afraid the answer to that question is *yes.*

I came to this conclusion three days ago as Carol and I sat out at the last Cubs game of the season and watched Andre Dawson belt his 399th career home run to give the Cubs a 3–2 victory. *Oy,* did we *kvell.* But what happened immediately after Dawson's home run? He jogs back out to right field—and the people in the bleachers bow down to him. Now what is the first commandment that Moses lugged all the way down with him from the top of Sinai? "I am the Lord your God; you shall have no other gods beside Me."

Is it any wonder, then, that the Cubs have not won a pennant, when their fans blatantly flout the first commandment? But what are we to do? Can we convince the fans in the right field bleachers that bowing down to Dawson is costing the Cubs a pennant? Not bloody likely. No, I have concluded, reluctantly, that for the Cubs to win a pennant they must let Andre Dawson go.

But I have some very bad news for us, even if the Cubs do trade Dawson. The second commandment says, "For I the Lord your God am an impassioned God, visiting the guilt of the fathers upon the children, upon the third and upon the fourth generations." So it looks to me like it'll be late 21st century—at the earliest—before we Cubs fans can hope for a pennant.

And they wonder why we Jews despair.

1993

Finishing Strong

Now, looking back, it seems like quite a feat that the 1993 squad managed the third winning season for the Cubs in twenty years. The front office allowed free agents Greg Maddux and Andre Dawson to slip away to the Atlanta Braves and the Boston Red Sox, respectively. Maddux had led the team in wins for five straight years; Dawson had led the team in RBIs for three—no major league team had ever before lost that combination of productivity. Maddux's alleged replacement, free agent Jose Guzman, formerly of the Texas Rangers, went just 12–10 on a tendinitis-afflicted shoulder; Maddux meanwhile went 20–10 for Atlanta. The Cubs were sucker-punched when Dawson's replacement, Candy Maldonado, another costly free agent, batted .186 before he was traded to the Cleveland Indians on August 8.

Given all that, an 84–78 record doesn't seem too bad. Heading into the final month of the season, the Cubs were six games below .500 and only 7½ above the expansion Florida Marlins. They then reeled off 20 wins in their next 28 games, due largely to the steady pitching of Greg Hibbard (15–11) and Jose Bautista (10–3), who combined for a 10–1 record in September. Free-agent acquisition Randy Meyers also chipped in 15 saves that month. He struck out 86 in just over 75 innings' work, and set a National League record with 53 saves for the year.

Meyers made the accusation in September that some of his team-mates weren't "winners," adding that "all they care about is their stats." He probably noticed burgeoning star Sammy Sosa's 33 home runs and 36 stolen bases, 20 of which came in a frantic last two months of the season. His 30/30 year was the first in Cubs history. But even with such gaudy numbers, Sosa batted a mediocre .261. He was widely thought to be too impatient and self-absorbed to meld his glamour stats into an all-around team contribution. Just wait.

Finding the Messiah

SOME OF YOU MAY HAVE NOTICED that we have a new rabbi this year.[1] Well I noticed that, too, and it seemed to me that he might like it if his congregants did not waste time on *Yom Kippur* talking about the Cubs. So I decided to talk about something serious, but not somber—not sports— at Open Mike this year. . . .

But then I got to thinking about it. I've been doing this for ten years now. It's become a tradition. And along comes a new rabbi and all of a sudden I shouldn't say what I want to say at Open Mike? Because we hired some big-shot clergy-man from the East, I should give up my First Amendment

---

[1] After a two-year search for a rabbi, the congregation hired Richard Hirsh. The comments about him in this talk are entirely untrue.

rights? Because he went to the Reconstructionist Rabbinical College in Philadelphia, and probably he's a Phillies fan, I should not mention the Cubs because it might—heaven forbid—offend our new rabbi? Y'know we weren't doing so badly around JRC without a rabbi for two years.

I'm not knocking the rabbi. His sermon about broken-ness last night was fine as far as it went—but what about the ground ball that went through Leon Durham's legs in the fifth game of the playoffs against the San Diego Padres in 1984, which shattered the dreams of millions of Cubs fans from Chicago to *Eretz Yisrael*? As you can imagine, the more I thought about it, the more upset I got at this new rabbi's *chutzpah,* coming in like this, destroying tradition, practically outlawing the Cubs as an institution. Where in the *Torah* does it say "no Cubs on *Yom Kippur,*" huh, show me? Fortunately, I've calmed down a little now. . . .

So anyway, I've been thinking quite a bit about the messiah lately. To tell you the truth, I've always been a little jealous of the Christians, they having found their messiah and all. Well, at least he was one of our boys. Or so they say. Me, I'm not so sure he was—a Jewish carpenter? But anyway, Jewish or not, he had some pretty good qualities for a messiah—kind, good values. Frankly, though, I don't think he was the real messiah.

Why? Well nowhere do we read—not even in the *New Testament,* where the Christians could have stuck in pretty much anything they wanted—nowhere do we read that Jesus was much of an athlete. And I'm almost certain that the messiah is going to turn out to be a pretty decent ballplayer.

By the way, for my fiftieth birthday last October, my
wife surprised me and took me to Cooperstown to visit the
Baseball Hall of Fame. Did you know that in 1912 a Cubs
player by the name of Henry "Heine" Zimmerman won the

triple crown, batting .372, hitting 14 home runs and driving in 106 runs? It's true.

There isn't, strictly speaking, a Jewish section to the Hall of Fame, but I can pretty much tell you where they all are—the plaques of Sandy Koufax, who won the Cy Young Award in 1963, '65 and '66, and Hank Greenberg, who hit 56 home runs. The balls from Kenny Holtzman's no hitters. *Oy*, did I *kvell*.

But back to the messiah. Y'know there is an old *Hasidic* notion that the messiah may come in an unexpected form, and so one should treat everyone he encounters as if that person were the *mashiach*. I've been thinking about that and I'd like to be the first to announce that I'm pretty sure I've spotted him.

As you know, this has been a pretty dismal year for the Cubs pitching staff, with one exception. There's a 29-year old, 6'2" right hander from the Dominican Republic named José Bautista. In 1992, José pitched for Omaha in the American Association and Memphis in the double-A Southern League, compiling a brilliant record of two wins and ten losses, with a 4.90 ERA. Naturally, the Cubs scouts see this and they figure, "Oh boy, this is the type of guy who's going to fit in real well on our pitching staff." So they sign him. And what does José do this year? He's got a 9–3 record, with a 2.82 earned run average.

And, are you ready for this? José Bautista is Jewish. Honest. A conservative Jew. His son, Leo, goes to Hebrew school. They light *shabbos* candles . . . So, it's like the *Hasidim* said, maybe you didn't expect the messiah to be a 6'2" Dominican pitcher, but who knows?

And if José should turn out to be the messiah, there'll be no problem on *Pesach*. I've tried it out, and I think José Bautista will fit nicely into the song, instead of *Eliahu: José Bautista-ha Navi*.[2] And, even if it doesn't fit, not to worry—I've got Bob Applebaum[3] working on a new melody, a Latin tune. Our cantor is going to have to learn to play the marimba with her *klezmer* band.[4]

Now, of course, I know that one season does not necessarily a *mashiach* make. But for a Jewish Cub fan, one good season by a Jewish pitcher is not exactly chopped liver, either. And the *Hasids* also say that we can't simply wait for the *mashiach*; we must do our part to bring him. So watch José. And when he comes in to pitch and doesn't give up any runs, do as I do—say a *shehehianu*.

---

2 Traditional Passover song.

3 JRC congregant and composer of many melodies sung by the congregation.

4 JRC's cantor at the time, Lori Lippitz, directed a klezmer group called The Maxwell Street Klezmer Band, which played traditional Jewish music.

1994

Strike

The strike of 1994 was a blight on the history of baseball. There was no World Series; the season was in fact over two-thirds of the way through; and fans had little reason to expect the best. It might be said that all of baseball had a typical Chicago Cubs year.

As for the beleaguered Northsiders, the strike might have been a blessing in disguise. The Cubs fell 16½ games out of first place in the National League Central Division in just 113 games, going 49–64, so it was doubtful that 49 more contests would have helped. The season was all but sunk anyway when the Cubs set a 20th century National League mark by losing their first 12 games at Wrigley Field. Their first home victory didn't come until May 4, when they beat the Cincinnati Reds 5–2. Steve Trachsel picked up the victory. He finished the truncated season 9–7 with an ERA of 3.21, winding up fourth in the NL Rookie of the Year voting.

Bad got worse on June 13, when second baseman extraordinaire Ryne Sandberg announced his retirement, saying he had lost the desire to play a game that was "no longer fun." At the time of his retirement, Sandberg was fourth on the team's all-time list in home runs (245), sixth in hits and seventh in RBIs. He also had a .990 career fielding percentage, the highest ever for his position.

But, like Michael Jordan, who left basketball for a brief time to pursue a baseball career, Sandberg would suit up again for the Cubs in 1996. Cubs fans returned to their places even more quickly. They were among the first fans in baseball to reach their old attendance numbers when the strike ended in 1995.

* *

The Bright Side of the Strike

ARE YOU THE SAME GROUP? I mean were all of you here last year? I hate to have to start all over again, with the same *mishigas* every year. Look, if you weren't here, you'll just have to ask somebody who was, okay?

I mean, I'm here every year. So why shouldn't you be? I put a hell of a lot of work into these talks. It's not something I just whip up after *Kol Nidre*, you know.

For example, on the second day of *Rosh Hashanah* last year I have to rush straight from services to Wrigley Field. This is not a pleasure trip; I'm on assignment. I have to figure out whether José Bautista, the Cubs Jewish pitcher from the Dominican Republic, is the messiah. So I called the Cubs office and told them I needed a press pass to get onto the field to talk to Bautista. It's true, here's my pass, and here's the autographed picture I got from José.

So I get down onto the field—Wrigley Field—the same field that Ernie Banks, Billy Williams, Phil Cavaretta, Hank

Sauer, Frankie Baumholtz, Harry Chiti[1] played on. Now, I don't know whether, technically, we Reconstructionist Jews believe in heaven, but I certainly do. I was there. There I am, mingling down on beautiful Wrigley Field among Mark Grace and Ryne Sandberg—not talking to them, mind you, I was much too excited for that, just mingling.

I spot Steve Stone; you know Steve Stone, the former Cy Young award-winning pitcher who is now the Cubs' announcer, the guy who corrects Harry Caray when he says "we're in the bottom of the 6th, fans, and the Cubs trail the Montreal Expos 4–3," when it's really the top of the eighth and the Cubs are ahead of the Florida Marlins, 7–2. Anyway, I see Steve Stone and I know that Stone is Jewish, and, remember, this is the second day of *Rosh Hashanah.* So I screw up my courage and I go over to Stone (who is smoking a disgusting cigar) and I stick out my hand and say, *"Shana Tova."* Steve looks at me kinda funny, then sticks his hand out and says, "Steve Stone." I am not making this up.

I know that at least some people listen to my open mike talks. Because this year Boris Furman, JRC's irrepressible social committee chairman, organized the first annual José Bautista Day at Wrigley Field. I'll admit, I wasn't sure how many people we'd get, just putting a small notice in the JRC newsletter. But I've got to hand it to Boris, there were over 34,000 people out there that day. We should sell advertising in the newsletter, and cut our membership dues in half.

---

[1] All former Cubs stars, except Chiti who was a mediocre catcher—and that's a generous assessment.

Anyway, José Bautista Day was a beautiful, sunny day. And the Cubs won, 3-0. And José didn't even have to pitch. God works in mysterious ways. By the way, I think the jury's still out as to whether José is the messiah. It's true his earned run average went way up this year. But, hey, even the messiah is entitled to an off year.

Of course, what weighs heavily on all of our minds this *Yom Kippur* is the baseball strike. I have searched my soul to see whether, perhaps, there was something I did to bring this upon us. Should I have been kinder to my children? Walked my dog, Rubovits, a few more times? But I concluded, no, I've been pretty-much perfect again this year. Why, then, I asked myself, why do we have this strike?

So, I did what I usually do when I am confronted by these kinds of existential questions, I turned to the *Torah*, which is actually a very good scroll, if you haven't read it lately. By the way, it's a good thing that they decided to put the *Torah* into book form. If you think it's hard to read the *Tribune* sports section on the El,[2] just imagine trying to scroll your way through *Leviticus* while the train lurches along.

But I digress. Anyway, turning to the *Torah*, I was reminded of all of the apparently horrible things that happened to the Jewish people that actually turned out to be really fortunate. I can't think of any examples of those things, off hand, but there are plenty of them in there, I'm sure.

Could it be, I wondered, that the baseball strike was actually

---

[2] El is short for "elevated," the public transportation that stops half a block from Wrigley Field.

good for the Jews or, what to me is the same thing, good for Cubs fans? So I looked back at last season's standings and I saw that the Cubs lost 78 games last year. This year, however, thanks to the strike, they lost only 64 games. That is the fewest games the Cubs have lost in a season since 1945. And, remember, this October will be the first time since 1945—forty-nine years—that Cubs fans will not have to watch two other teams play in the World Series. So let us give thanks as we say, *"baruch atah adonai eloheynu melech haolam,* who creates the baseball strike when enough is enough, already."

1995

Bouncing Back

If Rip Van Winkle had waited until September of 1975 to embark on his fabled nap, he would have awoken 20 years later to see that the 1995 Cubs finished 73–71, four games behind Colorado for the National League Wild Card spot.

Colorado? Wild Card? Cubs above .500? And didn't they use to play more games than this? Baseball underwent massive structural change and expansion in the 80s and 90s, but the progress the Cubs made in the year after the strike of '94 wasn't too shabby, either. Calling the pitiful '94 season on account of greed had been like euthanasia to the struggling Cubs. But shortening the '95 season by almost four weeks as the players' strike finally ended (explaining those 19 missing games) may have cost the Cubs a shot at their first post-season appearance of the decade. The club never fell out of the top few spots in their division and held first place for all but one day before June 4. They finally settled on third, their best finish since winning the division in '89.

Not bad for a team that sank quicker than a Greg Maddux forkball the previous season. The 24-victory improvement bumped them from the third-worst record in the majors to the sixth-best record in the National League—only four teams made a more dramatic turnaround. New manager Jim Riggleman surely had something to do with that, as did some shrewd early-season acquisitions, including 14-game winning right-hander Jaime Navarro and well-rounded outfielder Brian McRae. First baseman Mark Grace ranked fifth in the league with a .326 batting average and fell six doubles shy of tying the club record of 57 two-baggers in a season. Outfielder Sammy Sosa's rare combination of power and speed produced 36 home runs and 34 stolen bases. Sosa's second 30/30 year made him one of just six major-leaguers ever to achieve that feat twice in a career.

The franchise reached two milestones in '95. The Cubs became the first single-city major league franchise to win 9,000 games when Sosa launched a solo home run in the 13th inning to beat the Los Angeles Dodgers 2–1 on May 21. Twelve weeks later, also against the Dodgers, Sosa rapped the Cubs' 10,000th home run. Even sluggers as accomplished as Sosa don't often get to hit a 10-grand slam.

Forgiving Grudgingly

THIS HAS BEEN A YEAR of deep spiritual crisis for me. So I called the rabbi recently, to request a meeting.

"Is it urgent?" he asked.

"Sort of," I replied.

"May I ask what it concerns?"

"Well I suppose if you're going to help me, you'll have to

know what it concerns."

"I mean, may I ask over the phone?" he explained.

"Yes. It's baseball, the Cubs."

"*Oy vey*, then you'd better rush right over. How long do you think we'll need?"

"About four weeks," I estimated.

"Well, let me see, I have five *bar mitzvahs* scheduled, four weddings, three *brisses*, two funerals and a partridge in a pear tree. But I'll cancel them."

So I hied myself over to the *shul*. After we exchanged *shaloms*, the rabbi got straight to the point. "So, *nu?*" he asked.

"I've lost my faith," I said.

"I see that, it looks like you are becoming a Hare Krishna."

"No, I'm not becoming a Hare Krishna. I just happen to be getting bald, and you said to rush right over, so I didn't change out of my bathrobe and thongs."

"I see, then tell me, what seems to have caused this loss of faith?"

"The strike."

"The strike?"

"Yes, the baseball strike. I have lost interest in baseball."

"Lost interest? But what about Cal Ripken[1]?"

"*Ripken, Shmipken.* So he shows up every day for fourteen years. Big deal. If he'd been injured a couple days—or if his manager had made him take a day or two off, like he should have—nobody would know his name. Besides, we Jews have

---

[1] Baltimore third baseman Cal Ripken broke Lou Gehrig's record for consecutive games played.

had much longer streaks."

"What're you talking about?"

"Moses, in the desert, shows up 40 years in a row—14,600 consecutive days. And he didn't have an off season."

"But you've been such an avid Cubs fan . . ."

"I've lost interest in the Cubs, too. Usually, I go to twenty games a season. This year I went to two."

"But the Cubs were right in the thick of the wild card race. How could you have lost interest?"

"Oh, it's all a business, there's no sport anymore."

"But baseball's been a business for a long time. Surely you knew that before the strike."

"Yes, I knew it. We all knew it. But we pretended different. The strike destroyed all of our illusions."

"You sound very hurt, and angry."

"I am. That's why I came to you for advice."

"Well, you know what is coming up soon, don't you?"

"Of course I do, the World Series."

"No, I meant the High Holidays."

"Oh, yes, I forgot."

"And what are we Jews supposed to do for the Holidays?"

"Repent."

"Very good, that's right, and what else?"

"Unh-unh . . . oh no, I'm not forgiving. Besides, the offender is supposed to ask forgiveness, and the Cubs haven't asked me."

"Sure they did. Didn't they sell their tickets at half price through May?"

"A cheap trick to try to draw people in when the weather was lousy."

"You are being too harsh. Remember, God forgave the Israelites for building the Golden Calf, so can't you forgive the baseball owners and players for trying to slay the Golden Goose?"

So I have thought about what the rabbi said. And maybe I should forgive them; I don't know, I just don't know.

By the way, for those of you who may still be wondering, José Bautista is definitely not the messiah. He pitched for the San Francisco Giants this year, his earned run average soared to 6.44, and his record dropped to 3–8. Of course, in the off season, the Cubs will probably trade Mark Grace and Shawon Dunston to the Giants to get old José back.[2]

But, hey, how about that *Sammela* Sosa? I think maybe that big gold chain he wears around his neck has a *chai* on it.

Oh, what the heck; Rabbi, you're right . . . I forgive.

*La shana ha ba-a b'*Wrigley Field.

---

[2] The Cubs have a history of bad trades, perhaps the worst of which was trading budding superstar, Lou Brock, to the St Louis Cardinals for a pitcher who never amounted to anything, Ernie Broglio.

1996

A Bad Break

*The Cubs lost in 1996 because of bad pitching. Their pitchers set
a variety of records, from the positive, most strikeouts in a season
(1,027), to the opposite, most home runs allowed (184).*

*But, the Cubs' hopes for the year were dashed by a single pitch,
from Florida's Mark Hutton, that severely fractured Sammy Sosa's
hand on August 20. Catcher Scott Servais was hit by 14 pitches,
a club record, but it was the fastball to Sosa that sunk the Cubs'
season. Sosa had already belted 40 homers and driven in 100 RBIs
by that time, and, with his 18 stolen bases, was on pace to become
the first player since Willie Mays in 1955 to hit 50 home runs and
steal 20 bases in a season. He sat out with the busted paw until
1997, and the Cubs went from a scant 3½ games out of first place
on August 21 to 12 games out by the season's end, losing 14 of
their last 16 games and finishing fourth in the Central Division
with a record of 76–86.*

*Despite his early exit, Sosa was third among National League
outfielders with 15 assists, just one part of a defensively sound
team. The Cubs committed a National League-low 104 errors en*

route to a club-record .983 fielding percentage. Ryne Sandberg's return at age 36 after almost two years in retirement only bolstered those numbers. He ranked second among second basemen in fielding percentage, committed no throwing errors, and broke Rogers Hornsby's NL mark for career home runs at that position with his 265th. First baseman Mark Grace added a fourth Gold Glove to his trophy case and batted .331 for the year.

Clearly, the Cubs had talent. But by losing 34 one-run games and blowing a league-high 34 saves, the Cubs could only watch helplessly as the man they let get away, Greg Maddux, helped the Atlanta Braves win the World Series.

* *

Why Reconstructionists are Cubs Fans

I AM OFTEN ASKED TWO QUESTIONS: "Mr. Kanter, exactly what is the derivation of the modern *kippah*?" and "Why are all Reconstructionist Jews Cubs fans?" Well, as it happens, the two are closely related.

First, as to the derivation of the modern *kippah*. It is true that the *kippah*, when you examine it closely, is an odd garment. I mean, other than for a hair-challenged guy like me, what protection does it provide? Not much. So, are we to conclude that it had no useful purpose, ever? Not on your life, *bubbelah*. Listen up.

I have been studying the writings of the famous Jewish archeologist, Bernie Ha Levi. Bernie is accredited by most historians with the discovery of the Third Temple. Interviewed by *Time* magazine after his incredible discovery,

Bernie, in typical, self-effacing manner, said, "Hey, I figured they built one temple; somebody knocked it down. They built a second one; somebody knocked it down. So why would they stop at two?" It is Bernie who, in describing the dispersal of the Jews after the destruction of the Third Temple, coined the word "Triaspora."[1] But I digress.

Anyway, let me quote directly from page 398 of Bernie's archeological classic, *Holy Holes:*

"So I was digging and digging, and, whew, was it hot. I'm telling you, you think you know hot, you don't know hot, this was hot. So I come across something that looked like a *kippah*, except it had a long bill on it. And I say to myself, 'Hey, Bernie, wonder what this thing is?' I talk to myself a lot. Out loud. But that's neither here nor there. Well, actually, it was there.

"So, anyway, I start to put this thing on my head, until my wife, Ethel, who had packed a gorgeous picnic lunch for the dig—corned beef (extra lean), kosher pickles, a thermos of lattes, the whole schmear—said, 'Bernie, what are you, nuts, putting that on your head? That thing's filthy dirty. It's been buried in the ground maybe two, three thousand years.'"

"But it looks like a *kippah*," I said, "and it's got this bill on it."

"So? That means you've got to put that *schmutzig* thing on your head?"

So, I took the thing and smacked it against my hip a couple of times to sterilize it, and I began to inspect it more

---

[1] The Jews dispersal after the destruction of the second temple is referred to as the Diaspora.

carefully, and to speculate what it might have been used for. Then, suddenly, I shouted to Ethel, "Hey, Ethel, it is a *kippah*."

"How do you know that, Einstein?" Ethel asked.

"Because, look here, inside this one it says, in gold, 'Jesus' Bar Mitzvah, December 25, 13 C.E.' And, here's one that says, 'Maccabee Brothers Funeral Home,' and this one says, 'Abraham and Sarah's Wedding.'"

"But, if that's a *kippah*, why did they put a bill on it?" Ethel asked.

"Well, in the days of yore," I explained, "it was open air; they had no roof in the old temples. So during services, they probably needed something to keep the sun out of their eyes. Look, see, this one has sun glasses attached to the inside of the bill so you can flip them down."

Ethel inspected the front of the *kippah* closely and said to me, "Okay, genius, explain this to me. What's the big red C on the front for?"

Well I was temporarily stumped. I thought and I thought. Cardinals? No. Cleveland? No. Cubs? . . . No. Finally I figured it out and I said to Ethel, "Ethel, the C probably stands for Chosen. You know, we were the Chosen People."

"But why did they need a C on it? Everybody at the old temples was chosen."

"Sure, but the idol worshippers worshipped outside, also, and they had hats, too. So the Jews needed the C to distinguish them."

Anyway, further research by Bernie showed that once *shuls* were built with roofs on them, the bills had outlived their usefulness. So bills were cut off of *kippot* as a cost-saving measure. The *C* was dropped because, once services were moved indoors, all other religions had the good sense to drop *kippot* altogether (except the Pope, of course, who apparently didn't get the message), so there was no need to distinguish any more. And, so, that's the derivation of the modern *kippah.*

But why, then, you ask, are all Reconstructionist Jews Cubs fans? That's really quite simple. As you know, Mordecai Kaplan, our founder, in his great wisdom, decided to ditch the notion of chosenness altogether in our liturgy. But, deep down, we all want to feel chosen, even Reconstructionists. And so it is because of this deep, primeval connection we Reconstructionist Jews feel to the old Chosen *kippot* that we all are Cubs fans.

So, the next time you're out at Wrigley Field, and Harry[2] leads the singing in the seventh inning, remember, the correct words, "For it's root, root, root for the *Cho–sen,* if they don't win it's a *shanda* . . . "

*La Shana, ha ba-a b'*Wrigley Field.

---

[2] Cubs announcer, Harry Caray, who started the tradition of singing "Take Me Out to the Ball Game" as the fans stretched in the seventh inning.

1997

Retiring Fourteens

In the game-by-game record of the 1997 Cubs, the first 14 dates each have a capital L next to them. After the New York Mets mercifully lost to the Cubs on April 20 to end the streak, first baseman Mark Grace declared, "Thank God. We won a game. We're 1–14. That's atrocious, but I'm going to have a little fun tonight." Grace's candid, upbeat reaction no doubt stems from the fact that he had been a Cub his entire major league career.

That 14-game skid set the National League record for most consecutive losses to begin a season, and helped assure that the 1997 Cubs would not crawl above fourth place in their five-team division. They didn't win their lucky seventh game until May 2, by which time they had 22 losses, and settled into fifth place on June 8. When the St. Louis Cardinals beat them in the last game of the season, it was loss number 94, the most capital L's for the Cubs since 1980.

This season was probably not the farewell tour that Ryne Sandberg imagined when the legendary second-baseman announced his re-retirement on August 2, effective at the end of the year. He had been a Cub since 1981, for 2,151 games. In that stretch, he set major-league records for home runs (277) and fielding percentage (.989) at second base. Only one Cub had more stolen bases, three had more hits, and five had more RBIs. Sandberg was a 10-time All-Star, a 9-time Gold Glove recipient, and a likable guy, to boot.

After he won his MVP award in 1984, Sandberg's high school retired his number. No one who plays for North Central High School in Spokane, Washington will again wear number 14 on his uniform, just as no Cub player will ever again wear Mr. Cub's, Ernie Banks, number 14. And Cubs fans hoped to retire another 14; the 14-loss experience of 1997.

Kashering the Cubs

FIRST OFF, I WANT TO SAY that I don't think the Cubs had nearly as bad a season as most people think they did. The Bulls win 69 games and everyone is ecstatic. Well—big deal and whoop-de-do—the Cubs won 68 games. You say but the Cubs lost 83 more games than the Bulls. And I say, why do you always have to dwell on the dark side of everything? So it took the Cubs a few more games. Are you in such a big hurry? You're on your way to a fire or something? But, then, we Jews are used to this double standard, aren't we, so we shouldn't be so surprised when it's applied to our baseball team.

But, if you still think they had a bad year, consider this: in the first 14 games this season, the Cubs were 14 games under .500. In the next 148 games, though, they fell only another 12 games under .500. Talk about improvement. If they continue to improve at this rate, next season . . . should be a lot like this season.

Okay, so it wasn't such a great season. The question is why? I have a theory. Now I know that we Jews have a tendency to lapse into blaming ourselves for everything, into a kind of self-loathing. And I certainly don't want to fall into that trap. But my theory is that the Cubs are losing because we Reconstructionist Jewish Cubs fans are not taking the game seriously enough, not doing our part. To put it bluntly, instead of integrating our Judaism into baseball, we have forsaken baseball for *Torah*.

Let me give you a couple examples of how far we've fallen. How many of you remember the legendary Jewish pitcher, Sandy Koufax? Great. Now, tell me, how many of you can tell me the name of the Torah portion at Sandy Koufax's *bar mitzvah* and who catered the luncheon, afterwards? Uh-huh, I thought so. Okay, here's another one. How many of you can tell me the year that the Cubs last played in the World Series? No, not 1945; everyone knows that. The *Jewish* year.

But, you say to me, what about the Baltimore Orioles? They won their division this year. Did they have Jewish support? And why blame the Reconstructionists? What are the Orthodox doing? Well, I'm glad you asked.

I read to you now from the *Washington Post* on May 6, 1996 sent into me by an alert reader. And, as Dave Barry[1] would say, I am not making this up.

---

[1] Prolific and very funny humorist. I don't know whether he's Jewish.

It was the bottom of the fifth, two out, and the Orioles batter popped out to the catcher, ending a brief rally. As the O's took the field, a bit despondently, Saul Newman headed for a prayer session.

It had nothing to do with the fact that the Orioles were trailing badly and needed help, heavenly and earthly, in a game that was going south on them. Newman is an Orthodox Jew who prays three times a day, as custom prescribes, and he was heading off to join other Jews for their afternoon prayers in a small room behind the kosher food stand at Section 32 of Camden Yards.

The article also said, "a rabbi from Greenbelt wore an orange Orioles cap during the afternoon prayers, known as *mincha*." I'll bet the rabbi didn't even have a hat like mine that has the Cubs team name in Hebrew.[2]

But I digress. So, in Baltimore, they have a kosher food stand (potato *knishes* go for a buck seventy-five) and Jews praying, and the Orioles are winning big. It doesn't seem like much of a mystery to me as to what the Cubs need. And I'm going to fire off a letter to Cubs management to see if I can get the ball rolling. I have a couple ideas. For one thing, it occurs to me that, by now, maybe the Cubs old shortstop, Ivan de Jesus, has a kid who's ready to play major league ball. Wouldn't you just love to be a member of the Jews for de Jesus fan club? And another thing I think I'll suggest is that the Cub organization might help things along a little by hiring a general manager whose last name was not MacPhail.[3] How about the ex-pitcher, Early Wynn?[4]

Anyway, with these changes (and, of course, the kosher food and Mogen David wine vendors, and the new davening area in the center field bleachers), there's only one more thing we need to do—find a way to get to Harry Caray. Maybe we could do it through Steve Stone, who is an *MOT*.[5] Although, come to think of it, that may not be so promising. Most of you probably remember how in 1993, on my way off the field

---

[2] See the hat in the picture of the author on the back cover.

[3] Larry MacPhail, General Manager of the Cubs.

[4] Former Cleveland Indians and Chicago White Sox pitching great.

[5] Member of the Tribe, sometimes used to mean Jewish.

from interviewing José Bautista between *Rosh Hashanah* and *Yom Kippur,* I saw Steve Stone. I stuck my hand out and said, *"Shana Tova."* And, he paused a second, then put his hand out and said "Steve Stone." So maybe Steve's not our man.

But, why do we need to get to Harry, anyway, you ask? I would have thought that would be obvious to you—to convince Harry that in the seventh inning we ought to be singing, "For it's *echad, shtayim, shalosh* strikes you're out at the old ball game."[6]

*La shana, ha ba-a b'*Wrigley Field.

---

[6] Sadly, after 16 years as the Cubs announcer, Harry Caray died during the off season. A statue of him with his microphone, leading "Take Me Out to the Ball Game," now stands outside Wrigley Field.

1998

Caraying Out a Plan

In 1908, the last season the Cubs won the World Series, the entire
team hit 19 home runs. And, thirty years later, in 1938, they
managed just 65. Sixty years after that, though, in 1998, Sammy
Sosa alone belted 66 home runs.

Thus, the baton of Chicago's favorite athlete passed smoothly
in June—from Michael Jordan, who won a sixth world champion-
ship in his final game as a Chicago Bull, to Sammy Sosa, who hit
a major-league record 20 home runs that same month. Sosa's home
run tug-of-war with St. Louis Cardinal slugger Mark McGwire
captured the imagination of the nation. McGwire, who was first to
break Roger Maris' 37-year-old record of 61 home runs, didn't quit
until he hit 70. Sosa wound up with the second-highest total ever,
66, and added 158 runs batted in, for good measure.

Even more remarkable than the gaudy home run totals, though,
the Cubs were actually winning. And not just on account of Sosa's
hot bat. In only his fifth major league start, National League Rookie
of the Year Kerry Wood tied a major-league record by striking out 20
Houston Astros, a performance that Sports Illustrated *labeled the*
most dominant pitching performance ever. Reliever Rod Beck tested

Cubs fans' hearts all season, as he collected a club-record 51 saves.

It took a one-game playoff victory over the San Francisco Giants for the Cubs to earn a trip to the playoffs (for the first time in nine years); but there they were, in the postseason, as a Wild Card Team (what more fitting appellation for the Cubs than that?), battling the Atlanta Braves. Not surprisingly, the Braves swept the three games, restoring the Cubs to their rightful place in the order of the universe.

But the endearingly humble Sosa was the overwhelming choice as National League MVP. And the Cubs proved just as lovable as winners as they've always been as losers.

● ●

Glimpsing the Promised Land

WOULD LIKE TO SPEAK TODAY about maturity.

I am not a mature person. While my wife and daughters would point to hundreds of examples to prove this beyond any reasonable doubt, I prefer not to wallow in those reasons today. Instead, I would like to focus on just one—the Chicago Cubs.

To give me my due, I've made progress. Not long ago, my moods could swing dramatically with a Bulls or a Bears win or loss. Now, frankly, I couldn't care less whether the Bulls play this year. And about the only thing I'd sorta like to see in the remainder of the pro football season is Mike Ditka[1] lose all the rest of his games.

---

[1] Former head coach of the Chicago Bears, now coach of the New Orleans Saints. A brash, controversial figure—and not my favorite person.

It's just the Cubs I care about now. I'll grant you that I may take this to extremes. About a month ago, for example, we got a new puppy to go with our main dog, Rubovits. My wife, Carol, and I disagreed over what to name the puppy. Ultimately, I prevailed by making Carol a deal—if Sammy hit a home run that day, we'd name the puppy Sosa. Not that the other name we were considering, Wrigley, would have been so bad either.

But, I do not spend my time watching Cubs games frivolously. For me, it is an intensely Jewish experience. For starters, I always wear my Hebrew Cubs hat. Let me give you a few more examples of what I mean by a Jewish experience.

On June 5, in the seventh inning of the Cubs–White Sox game, I found myself pondering why the blessing over the wine did not read simply, *"Baruch atah adonai, eloheinu melech haolam, shenatan lanu yayin."* "Blessed are you, God, who has given us wine." Not atypically, the Cubs had blown a 5–2 lead. With the game tied and a runner on first, the Sox batter hit a shot to right center, and, as the runner on first rounded third with what would have been the winning run, the ball stuck in the ivy. The Sox runner was sent back to third and the Cubs won the game in the 12th inning, with a home run. An epiphany struck me: the blessing over the wine, *boray p'ree hagafen*—who has given us the fruit of the vine—was originally (and, properly understood, is still today), a baseball blessing for Cubs games at Wrigley Field.

Another significant game for me was the August 24 game against the Houston Astros. Some of you may recall the driving rain that day, a flood of Biblical proportions, that delayed the game almost two hours. A couple weeks before that game, anticipating a spiritual crisis on the 24th, I had called our new rabbi to ask if he would counsel me at Wrigley Field. Selflessly, he accepted.

While, of course, I can't tell you everything that Rabbi Rosen and I discussed, much of which was incredibly personal—and I'd be the last to reveal all that he confided in me—I can tell you that a portion of our time was spent discussing the arcane, but extremely important, question—much debated in the Talmud—of how one converts from being a Colorado Rockies fan to a Cubs fan.[2] The answer is that it takes three things: intense study of former Cubs greats, especially Jewish players like Ken Holtzman[3] (fortunately for the rabbi, it's a short list); attending a *bat din*[4] (which is the noise created by a lot of Cubs hits); and a trip to the *mikva* at the Cubby Bear.[5] I am working assiduously with the rabbi, and hope to have his conversion completed by opening day, 1999.

Then, on September 13th, Carol, Jodi, and I saw Sammy Sosa's 61st and 62nd home runs, against the Brewers. Though that wasn't, as they say in baseball, chopped liver, even better was the Cubs rally from way back to tie the game in the 9th and then win it in the 10th on a home run by Mark Grace—

---

[2] Rabbi Brant Rosen, an avid baseball fan, moved to JRC from Denver, where he was a partial season ticket holder of the Colorado Rockies.

[3] Former Cubs pitching star who threw two no-hitters.

[4] A beit din is a panel of rabbis who, among other things, validate a conversion.

[5] A watering hole for Cubs fans, near Wrigley Field.

get this—on Gracie the Swan Beanie Baby Day. Is that the definition of *bashert*, or what?

Jewish experiences are not all so rosy, though. On September 23, I watched the entire Cubs-Brewers game on TV. Had you been in my house that afternoon, you would have thought that at least one person had died when you heard me screaming at the TV, "NO! NO! NO!" as Brant Brown[6]

---

[6] A young Cubs outfielder. The fly ball he dropped cost the Cubs the game, and almost cost the team the Wild Card position.

dropped the last out, allowing three runs to score. Of course, silent between my "NO! NO! NO!" were the words "NOT AGAIN! NOT AGAIN! NOT AGAIN!" Immediately, in my misery, I pulled out and reread the *Book of Job*.

Finally, two nights ago at Wrigley Field, in the playoff game for the wild card spot, I glimpsed the Promised Land, as the Cubs beat the Giants 5–3. I may never get there but, hey, neither did Moses.

To further show the progress I'm making toward maturity, today, on *Yom Kippur*, I'd like to forgive two people publicly. First, Brant Brown for dropping that fly ball. How can I continue to harbor a grudge against a ball player who is about the same age as my two daughters? And besides, it was Brant Brown who hit the winning home run in the 12th inning against the White Sox in the *boray p'ree hagafen* game on June 5. And second, I'd like to forgive our rabbi for having the same first name as Brant Brown.

But in another sense, as I admitted earlier, I am not a mature person. I still care deeply about the Cubs. I still love few things better than being out at Wrigley Field. I think maturity is grossly overrated, anyway. I'm hoping never to reach it completely—and I think I've got a damn good shot at achieving that goal.

There have been times when I've wondered whether talking about the Cubs on *Yom Kippur* was an irreligious thing to do. It's not. Can you image a more spiritual experience than walking into Wrigley Field on a sunny afternoon, seeing the green of the grass and the ivy on the walls, and sitting among a true community of 38,000 people who exude nothing but love towards a multiracial group of men who they are pretty darn sure are ultimately going to lose?

In closing, I'd like to repeat what Sammy Sosa said, in another language, *"Kadur basis tov meod, tov meod aylai."*[7]

*L'Shana Ha ba-a b'*Wrigley Field.

---

[7] "Baseball's been very, very good to me."

1999

End of a Millennium (at last)

On June 8, the Cubs seemed poised to repeat their 1998 success. Nine games above .500, just a game and a half out of first place in the National League Central, the veteran Cubbies looked loaded and ready for another playoff run.

For some teams, though, that shoe doesn't fit. For the Cubs, it was their Sox that gave them fits.

After taking two of three from the hot Arizona Diamondbacks in Phoenix, the Cubs returned to Wrigley Field to host their cross-town rivals, the Chicago White Sox. The Cubs dropped three straight to the Sox. Then they dropped off the face of the planet by losing 59 of their next 84 games.

Included in that Chernobylesque melt-down was an all-time franchise low 6–24 record in August and an equally ignominious 2–10 out of the blocks in September. The team that was flirting with .600 shortly after Memorial Day needed their own memorial service by Labor Day.

The season may have been doomed when 1998 Rookie of the Year Kerry Wood was lost for the year—and potentially his career—with an elbow injury. Closer Rod Beck, another 1998 hero, was out for most of the season with bone spurs in his elbow, then was traded to the Red Sox.

As usual, the season had its bright spots. Sammy Sosa became the first major league player in history to hit 60 home runs in two consecutive seasons, though Mark McGwire ultimately exceeded Sammy's 1999 total of 63 home runs by two. Cubs first baseman Mark Grace garnered a total of 1754 hits in the 90s, more hits than any other player in the decade. Finishing second to Grace was an outfielder the Cubs traded away to the Texas Rangers, Rafael Palmeiro, thus reminding Cubs fans one last time of the century that might have been.

Is God a Cubs Fan?

S WE MEET, THE CUBS are 60–89, 31 games out of first, and possessors of the third worst record in all of baseball. A season like the one we're suffering through tests a Cub fan's faith—and stupidity. I score high in both tests.

The season also causes thoughtful folks (like me, for instance) to raise important, serious questions; questions that may challenge assumptions we've made all our lives; assumptions so strong we may not even have been aware we've made them. I'd like to discuss one such assumption today by asking, "Is God a Cubs fan?"

But before I do, I'd like to put to rest another question that we left hanging last *Yom Kippur,* a question that may have been troubling many of you (consciously or not) throughout this season. You'll recall that shortly before the 1998 High Holidays, Rabbi Brant Rosen arrived on our doorstep from Denver, an open and notorious partial-season ticket holder of the Colorado Rockies. Immediately, I began his conversion. Brant took well to his exposure to Wrigley Field in late 1998 and studied intensely to become a Cubs fan in the off season.

Before the 1999 season, Brant called me and reported that he had become a Cubs fan. Now I don't want you to think that I don't trust our rabbi, but I was trained as a lawyer and I don't trust anybody. So I conceived of a simple plan to test him. On May 4, I invited Brant out to a Cubs-Rockies game. During the game, I scrutinized his every move. He *kvelled* when the Cubs scored 4 runs in the third, 3 in the fourth and 1 in the fifth to take an 8–2 lead. He grimaced when the Rockies retaliated with 3 in each of the sixth, seventh and eighth to go ahead 11–8. He was on his feet when the Cubs tied it 11–11 in the bottom of the eighth. He consoled me when the Cubs gave up a run in the top of the ninth, and he whooped (as best a rabbi can whoop) when the Cubs scored two in the bottom of the ninth to pull it out, 13–12. So I can report confidently that Brant's conversion is complete. Sorry about that, Rabbi.

But it does not necessarily follow that because Brant is a Cubs fan God must be, too. As a recovering lawyer, I can see the fallacy in this reasoning. Indeed, we need to step back and ask, preliminarily, whether God is a baseball fan at all. The answer to that question is—of course God is a baseball fan. I

mean I'm willing to revisit fundamental assumptions, but let's not get ridiculous here, okay? God not a baseball fan? Get real.

Now that we've established that God is a baseball fan, the question remains—for whom does he root? Perhaps, you may suggest, he does not root for any team. After all, he is the God of all baseball fans; our pain is his pain, so to speak. But remember that God sees all, which means he has season tickets for all 30 teams. (Pretty good seats, too. Between home and first, except in Wrigley Field. It seems that after the Cubs last pennant in 1945, God forgot to renew on time for the 1946 season, and they stuck him way down the right field line, beyond the visitors' bull pen). But I digress . . . can you imagine how boring it would be for God to watch every baseball game and not have a team to root for?

But which team? Fortunately, we can eliminate certain teams confidently, right off the bat. For example, in Mordecai Kaplan's weighty tome, *Judaism as a Civilization*,[1] a little-noted passage that appears right after the section in which Kaplan debunks the notion that the Jews are God's chosen people says, "And the notion that God might be a Yankees fan must be repugnant to every modern Jew." I mean even Kaplan drew the line somewhere.

And certainly God would not root for a team in a domed stadium. Where's the connection to heaven there, I ask you? Nor could he be a fan of a new team, such as the Arizona Diamondbacks or the Tampa Bay Devil Rays. For whom would he have been rooting all those years before those teams came along? And God's not going to back a team that offends Native Americans; so, poof, there go the Braves with their tomahawk chant and the Cleveland Indians, the tribe.

Unfortunately, I don't have time to run through all thirty

---

[1] The central writing of the founder of Reconstructionism.

teams, because the 3-minute time limit for Open Mike talks is being strictly enforced this year. So let me cut to the chase. Ultimately, it comes down to two teams. God could be either a Cubs fan or a Boston Red Sox fan. Indeed, sometimes those two teams seem indistinguishable. Both play in great old ball parks, neither has won a World Series in over 80 years, Cubs first baseman Leon Durham blew the 1984 pennant by letting a ground ball go through his legs and ex-Cubs first baseman Bill Buckner blew the World Series for the Red Sox with an error two years later.

How do we determine, then, whether God is a Cubs fan or a Red Sox fan? Simple: we do as the ancients did, we look for a sign. So all season long I sat out at Wrigley Field thinking, "Please God, give me a sign." I really concentrated on it, hard, "Please, God," I said to myself, "give me a sign. Are you a Cubs fan?" I watched everyone carefully for that sign—the coaches (who do give signs), the players, the fans, the umpires, the ushers, the beer vendors—everyone. When the seventh inning stretch came, I kept expecting the Cubs public address announcer, Paul Friedman, a Jew, to say, "Leading us in 'Take Me Out to the Ball Game' today will be the biggest Cubs fan of them all, *Ha Shem*."[2] And a deep, resonant voice would emanate from the booth, saying, "Okay, let me hear you, good and loud, *echad, shtayim, shalosh* . . ."

But none of that happened and I was beginning to despair.

---

[2] In tribute to former Cub announcer Harry Caray, a celebrity guest now leads the singing of this song each game.

I thought I might have to wait until Sunday, September 26, for the last game in Wrigley Field this millennium—Millennium Beanie Baby Day for heaven's sake—for God's fandom to be revealed. I thought that until this Saturday, that is. (For those of you wondering why I was out at Wrigley Field on *shabbos,* let me remind you that it was a 3:05 PM start and a Reconstructionist Cubs fan is permitted to go to any game on *shabbos* provided that *shabbos* will be over—that is, the ballpark lights will come on—before the end of the game). So there I was in the sixth inning, when Sammy became the first player ever to hit 60 home runs in two seasons. And those of you who were there, or saw the replays on TV, you know what *Sammela* did as he rounded the bases. Yes, he pointed up at the sky, saluting the greatest Cubs fan of them all.

*L'millennium ha ba-a b'*Wrigley Field.

2000

Turning Back the Clock

Of great concern to computer owners in late 1999 was the Y2K glitch, which would supposedly cause digital clocks to interpret 2000 as 1900. After a seamless technological transition to the new year, though, it appeared that only the Cubs had been afflicted: their paltry 65 wins matched the team's total in 1900. If history is actually repeating itself, the Cubs are on course to lose the World Series to the White Sox in 2006, win the next two Series, then never be heard from again. At times the organization did seem intent on turning back the clock, in order to push something—anything— forward. It replaced manager Jim Riggleman and his 374–419 record with the old-school Don Baylor, the former Colorado Rockies manager who, as a player, placed himself in harm's way often enough to be hit by a major league record 267 pitches. Baylor-the-manager promptly exposed himself to getting beaned by challenging star slugger Sammy Sosa to improve his defense and baserunning. Sosa groused publicly, but did round out his game, and for good measure hit a league-high 50 home runs. By July, his career home run total surpassed Joe DiMaggio's 361—though Sosa's strikeouts outnumbered DiMaggio's nearly four-to-one.

Old faces returned (Joe Girardi from the Yankees, Kerry Wood from surgery) but they were few. The Cubs used a team-record 51 players throughout the season, and only five of those had played on the 1998 playoff squad. After winning their opener in Tokyo over the Mets, the Cubs sank fast, to 5th place by the All-Star break. From that point until the end of July, they rebounded to win 14 of 18 (can they? might they?) before losing 44 of their last 58 (nah). For the first time in major league history, no team finished above .600, not even the repeat champion Yankees, and no team finished below .400. With their 65-97 mark, the Cubs landed at .401.

* *

Mr. Cub, the Dalai Lama and the First Lady

WELCOME TO CHAPTER ONE OF volume two. I'm thinking about calling the sequel "The Son of God is a Cubs Fan," but that title has some obvious problems. Fortunately, though, we've got another fifteen years to work the kinks out.

And, speaking of working on a title, this obviously was not the Cubs' year. But, if you think we Cubs fans are long suffering because we have not won a World Series in 92 years, consider this. Greek runner, Konstantinos Kenteris, won the 200-meter sprint in the Olympics in Sydney this year. According to Bob Costas, the last Greek to win an Olympic sprint before Konstantinos was in 269 A.D. So, Cubs fans, quit your *kvetching.*

Personally, I think the Cubs made a big strategic mistake before the season even started. As you remember, they played their first two regular season games in Japan against the Mets. Anyone who has ever traveled that far knows how much a trip like that can take out of you. After their return from Japan, the Cubs were promptly crushed by the Cardinals in their next three games. Some would argue that they never recovered from the Japan trip.

If they'd asked me, I would have advised the Cubs to stay home and forfeit the first two games. Big deal, it would have cost them one game. Instead of being a wiped-out 1-1, they would have been a well-rested 0-2. Besides, think about how much fun it would have been to watch Mike Piazza and the other Mets running around Tokyo alone, eating sushi and trying frantically to find somebody to play. The trouble with the Japanese explanation for the Cubs' failure, though, is that the Mets made the playoffs.

Of course, the biggest trauma of this season was the prospect of the Cubs trading Sammy Sosa to the Yankees—for two pretty decent eighth-grade pitchers. For me, that trade presented a serious personal problem. Those of you who have been coming to these Open Mikes regularly—and paying attention—know that our younger standard poodle is named Sosa. (By the way, I'm proud to announce that Carol and I are grandparents. Sosa-the-dog had a litter of five puppies this year. *Oy*, such *nachas*. But, in case any of you think that I'm somebody you'd want to mess around with, I should tell you that shortly after their birth I promptly sold all five of our grandchildren. But I digress). So, anyway, there I was, facing the prospect of owning a dog named after

a Yankee outfielder. Clearly, this would be intolerable, so I
began training Sosa-the-dog to respond to what I decided
was going to be her new name—Steinbrenner.[1] (I actually
think that Steinbrenner is a cute name for a dog. It would
have gone well with Rubovits, our other poodle. Rubovits, by
the way, was the father of Sosa's puppies. Okay, so we've had
a bit of scandal in the Kanter family this year. But I digress
again). It's hard to blame the Cubs' season on Sosa-the-
ballplayer, though, with his 50 home runs, 138 runs batted in
and .320 batting average.

But this has been the year-of-the-book for me. Even before
Is God a Cubs Fan? was published, Rabbi Rosen presented
me with a gift that has become my most prized possession,

---

[1] George Steinbrenner is the owner of the Yankees.

a photo of Ernie Banks, inscribed "To Arnie. God is a Cub fan. Ernie Banks." After the *minyan* services at which Brant gave me the photo, I was talking to Hallie Rosen, who likes baseball, but is not a nut about it. As I was running on and on, trying to explain to her the magnitude of the gift that had just been bestowed upon me, Hallie interrupted me politely to say, "Well, I had some idea that it was important, because Brant got an autographed picture, too, and he has his displayed right next to the photo taken of him with the Dalai Lama." That seems to me about right. I'll bet the Dalai Lama tells his fans, "Let's pray two today."

I hope that many of you were able to attend the wonderful party thrown at JRC in December to celebrate publication of *Is God a Cubs Fan?* It was JRC at its best. How many congregations do you know that would allow bleachers to be set up in the main sanctuary, or have their choir sing "Take Me Out to the Ball Game" in Yiddish? A young non-Jewish friend of ours who attended said in awe, "It was like a rock concert."

Of course, *Is God a Cubs Fan?* is now popular around the world. Carol and I took a combination bike trip/book tour to China this May and were gratified at how the Chinese flocked to hear my readings. We later found out that the Hebrew letters for Cubs on my hat also mean "free mu shu pork" in Chinese.

And, of course, you have all heard about the letter I received from Hillary Clinton, on White House stationery. She wrote, "Thank you for the copy of *Is God a Cubs Fan?* which I received through the kindness of our mutual friend,

Eli Segal. It is a theological question I have asked myself many times and I am glad that you chose to devote your amusing little book to a problem that has perplexed me from girlhood. It might give you some comfort to know that Methodists all over the North Side have been asking the same question for years."

My friend Eli told me recently that Hillary's chief of staff said that Mrs. Clinton insists on carrying *Is God a Cubs Fan?* with her when she campaigns in New York. Hillary says she needs the Hebrew and Yiddish glossary at the back of the book. So the next senator from New York may owe JRC, big time.

In preparing for *Yom Kippur,* though, I came to ponder seriously whether my book itself was the cause of the Cubs' dismal year? Had I, perhaps, offended The Big Cub Fan, and was He not only visiting another plague upon the Jews by giving the Cubs the worst record in baseball, but adding insult to injury by causing the White Sox to win their division?

But I have rejected that theory. After all, if God were angry and punishing the Jews because of the book, surely I, as the author, would bear the brunt of the suffering. Yet, of the 21 Cubs games I went to this season, the Cubs won 14 of them. The odds against somebody attending 21 Cubs games this year and seeing them win 14 are 33:1 (somebody actually calculated this for me), which is statistically significant. So, if God is pissed about the book, He's showing it in an odd way.

And the fact is, I feel really good this *Yom Kippur.* Why, you ask, should I feel so good when the Cubs had such a miserable season? Obviously, if you ask this question, you just don't get the High Holidays. Each year we Jews gather together to recognize our shortcomings in the past year. We know that perfection is not attainable. Indeed, we expect to be back repenting again next year. All we seek is to improve. I ask you now, who has a better chance of improving next year than a team that finished with the worst record in baseball, 32 games under .500 and 30 games out of first place in their division? To analogize this to the game of Monopoly, this season for Cubs fans is like getting a "Get Out of *Yom Kippur* Free" card for next year. Is it any wonder my spirits are soaring?

2001

Bonds for Glory

2001 will be the year people remember baseball in spite of themselves. There was just too much: Barry Bonds' prodigious offensive season, a summer with the Boston Red Sox and Cubs both in first place, the owners' vote to eliminate two teams, and Ichiro-mania, over the veteran Japanese outfielder who became the American League rookie of the year. The Seattle Mariners tied the 1906 Cubs' major league record of 116 wins in a season. Then, like those self-same Cubs, they were bounced from the playoffs, dismissed by the New York Yankees. The Yankees in turn lost the World Series to a four-year-old franchise, the Arizona Diamondbacks, whose bottom-of-the-ninth, Game 7 comeback was spurred by Mark Grace and Luis Gonzalez, ex-Cubs both. That game ended Nov. 4, the latest World Series ever, because baseball's season paused for a week after the Sept. 11 attacks on New York and Washington, D.C. The sight of police and firefighters hurtling into flaming skyscrapers excised terms like "heroic" from the parlance of sport.

Within the context of the game of baseball, though, the seasons of the overachieving Minnesota Twins, Philadelphia Phillies, and, yes, Chicago Cubs were gutty, if not heroic. The Cubs managed to hold onto the National League Central lead until late August, when a gradual meltdown took them to a respectable third place, only five games out of first. That despite a couple of promising acquisitions (Fred McGriff, Michael Tucker), some of the best starting pitching in the NL and the finest overall offensive year of Sammy Sosa's career.

In November, San Francisco's Bonds was named Most Valuable Player, but tellingly, the two first-place votes he didn't get were those of the Chicago newspapers' beat writers, and both of those went to the season's real MVP—Sosa.

Counter-terrorism

THIS IS NOT A FUNNY TIME. As such, it seems highly inappropriate to deliver an Open Mike talk about the Cubs. What does baseball have to do with life, post September 11th, anyway? So, I think this year I'm just going to leave it at "*Shana Tova*". . . .

But that's exactly what they want, isn't it? Evil people have been trying to sabotage my Open Mike talks for years. But they underestimate my resolve. I say to all of them today, "Make no mistake about it, I will not be cowed into silence. Neither will I be sheeped nor rammed into silence."

This year, I decided to keep a Cubs diary. Though that diary is intensely personal, I am going to read most of it to you today.

Monday, April 2nd

Dear Diary:

I go to opening day, optimistic. It's a brand new season, and we've got our ace pitcher, Jon Lieber, on the mound. I just know that this is going to be our year. I settle into my seat with my Hebrew National kosher hotdog as Lieber winds up and delivers his first pitch, which is lined into right field for a single. Fine, no problem; this removes the pressure of a no-hitter. Lieber throws his next pitch, which is belted for a home run into the right field bleachers. Great, two pitches into our brand new season, and we're down 2–0. The Cubs lose 5–4 in 10 innings.

Tuesday, April 3rd

Dear Diary:

A good day. The Cubs don't play.

Wednesday, April 4th

Dear Diary:

Kerry Wood, our other great pitching hope, is on the mound today. Again, I am filled with anticipation. In the first inning, Wood gives up three runs. So our two ace pitchers now have a combined earned run average of 22.5 for the first inning. In the bottom of the ninth inning, Sammy Sosa is picked off of first base, with the tying run on third base and only one out. The Cubs lose, 3–2. In the first two games, they have now left a total of 21 runners on base.

Dear Diary:

Forget it. I am quitting this diary. It's too damn depressing.

As some of you may know, at the JRC benefit last March, I auctioned off two tickets to a Cubs game with Rabbi Rosen and me. So, on May 1st, the rabbi and I meet Sam and Jake Zivin at the Dempster Street el station. By this time, the Cubs are in first place, with the best record in the National League. We just miss a train at Dempster; not a good sign. In the third inning, Cubs pitchers issue four walks and the Padres score seven runs on only three hits; 7–0 Padres. In the next inning, the Padres add three more runs; it's now 10–0. The rabbi has a Bud Light. So, there we are, in the bottom of the fourth inning, left with only two hopes—that God will bring forth a downpour of Biblical proportions, or that the Cubs will score a touchdown and a field goal to tie the score. Neither of those hopes pans out.

To make matters worse, in the fourth inning, Cub relief pitcher, Mike Fyhrie, gets hit with the top half of a broken bat, and breaks his arm. The only positive note in the entire evening is that all four of us JRCers punch our all-star ballots for a straight ticket of Jewish ballplayers—Shawn Green, Mike Lieberthal, Gabe Kapler, Scott Schoeneweis, Scott Radinsky, Keith Glauber, David Newhan, Al Levine, and Brad Ausmus. We are careful to leave no hanging chads on the ballots.

Two weeks later, on May 15, I pick up the Chicago *Tribune*. Sports columnist Rick Morrissey has posed the following question to his readers: "If God said through His state-of-the-art public-address system, 'The Cubs will win the World Series this season, but as part of the deal I am proposing Wrigley Field will be torn down and not replaced afterward,' would you agree to the offer?"

The *Trib* does not print my reply. Fortunately, I have other ways:

"Dear Rick:

You have posed a false dilemma. Surely, you have read the story in the Bible of God calling upon Abraham to sacrifice his son Isaac. In the end, God was testing Abraham's faith, and provided a ram in Isaac's stead. After all, what kind of a God would ask for such a sacrifice?

"Similarly, by asking Cubs fans if they would sacrifice Wrigley Field for a World Series, God would be posing

another test of faith, and He would provide another ram—
Sox Park, which should be razed. And the Cubs would go on
to win the World Series in Wrigley Field, the Promised Land,
where they belong. After all, what kind of a God would ask
for such a sacrifice?"

By the way, it figures, doesn't it, that this year, when the
Cubs finally will be playing baseball well into the month of
October, you're going to have to play into November in order
to win the World Series? To paraphrase something I used to
be told in my youth, it's almost as if somebody is saying to
us, "Yeah, sure, the Cubs will win the World Series—come
Chanukah in the Vatican."

But what does baseball have to do with life, post September
11th? One week after the attacks, the Cubs played their first
game. Though, normally, I'd have been watching from the
first pitch, I tuned in half-heartedly in the ninth inning and
watched the Cubs give up three runs and lose, 6–5. What did I
do? I simply turned the set off. I did not cry. I did not curse.
I threw nothing at my TV.

So, what does baseball have to do with life, post September
11th? Perhaps at least this: baseball may serve as a kind of
barometer of normalcy. When any of us can really care again
about who wins a game, or a pennant, or the World Series,
perhaps, then, we will have begun our healing. I pray that
that day may come soon.

2002

The Don's Last

The Cubs in 2002 were all about strikeouts. The Cubs' staff led the National League in Ks as their top two starters, Kerry Wood and Matt Clement, each struck out more than 200 batters, only the second time two Cubs pitchers accomplished that feat. And rookie pitcher Mark Prior, the second pick in the draft, became the first Cub in 43 years to strike out 10 batters in his debut with the team. Then again, the lineup also led the Major Leagues in strikeouts, with Sammy Sosa characteristically setting the pace with almost one per game. He enjoyed another scintillating individual season nonetheless, leading the National League in home runs (49) and runs (122) and finishing the season with 499 career homers. The only Cub to match Sosa's strikeout total was free-swinging Mark Bellhorn, who wasn't much for a batting average but who did, against Milwaukee, become the first player to homer from both sides of the plate in one inning.

Mostly the team swung and missed, losing 17 of its first 25 games and floating face-down all season. After a 34-49 start in which the Cubs proved offensively inept, team management canned

Don Baylor, the Cubs' manager since 2000. Cubs president Andy MacPhail justified the move by saying, "the talent on the field does not equal the amount of victories in the standings." Up from the team's Triple-A farm team came Bruce Kimm, who demonstrated that if the team did possess hidden talent, it would take someone else to find it. He piloted the team to a Bayloresque 33-46 mark the rest of the way.

The Cubs finished in fifth place, 30 games behind division-leading St. Louis. The Cardinals went on to lose to San Francisco Giants in the National League Championship Series, and the Giants in turn lost to the Anaheim Angels in the World Series. Those were the days of rally monkeys and an overall élan to the game. Once more, the Cubs could only watch October baseball from afar, but it turned out San Francisco's loss would be their gain.

A Tough Season for God

THIS HAS NOT BEEN A good season. In fact, as it is said in the Talmud, it has sucked.

To recap briefly, by mid-May things already look grim. So, on Thursday, May 23, a group of four selfless JRCers set out for the right field bleachers to try to coax the Cubs out of their doldrums. Now I'm not going to name names here, but one of the group has the initials BR, and he's a rabbi. Arriving an hour before game time and undeterred by a heavy rainstorm, we meet at the Harry Caray statue, assume our seats in the bleachers and begin to sell copies of *Is God a Cubs Fan?* to bleacherites, netting three sales and a cool forty-five bucks for JRC.

The Cubs are equally successful. They score eleven runs and win, 11–6. Sosa, McGriff and Alou together have six hits in thirteen at bats, including one home run, five singles, four runs batted in and five runs scored. Not bad, but if the Cubs had traded Sosa, McGriff and Alou for one Jewish guy they'd have done a lot better. On that same day, Shawn Green alone hit four home runs, a double and a single, drove in seven runs and scored six.

By mid-August, the Cubs have sunk to new lows, even for them. They are last in the National League in batting and first in the league in strikeouts. They have lost 39 games by either one or two runs. The bullpens' ERA for August, excluding Joe Borowski, is 9.82.

By *Erev Rosh Hashanah*, the Cubs are more than twenty games under .500, and there are only two questions on congregants' minds. Why is it so damn hot in the church, and is God still a Cubs fan?

So, between Rosh Hashanah and Yom Kippur, I spring into action to try to answer the second question. I call God. I do this reluctantly, because I know He's busy inscribing people into the books of life and death. But I need to talk to Him.

My call confirms that in fact there is one God. Even the phone number suggests this – 1-800-adonai-1. But the first menu proves it absolutely, "press one if you're Catholic, two if you're Protestant, three if you're Buddhist, four if you're Baptist, five if you're Methodist, six if you're an Atheist…" Finally you get to "press eighteen, chai, if you're a

Reconstructionist."

I'm put on hold, and I get some background music, which I recognize immediately as Bob Applebaum's[1] setting of *Sh'hu Noteh Shamayim*. A recording tells me, "El Shadai

is busy dealing with other kvetches, but please stay on the line because your call is so important to Him, you wouldn't even believe it, Boychick." I am told that I may be able to get a quicker response by logging onto adonaieloheynu.org. I have to admit that the fact that my call may be monitored "for quality control purposes" does not exactly enhance my confidence in the Infallible One.

Finally, He answers, "Yo, Adonai here, how may I bless you and your offspring?"

"I'm calling about the Cubs."

"*Oy-a-brach*, I'm so sorry."

"You're sorry? What's that supposed to mean? You're God, why don't you do something about it?"

"I tried, I sent them Moses."

"You sent them Moises. And he started off the season on the

---

[1] Applebaum, a JRC member and composer, has written many melodies used by the congregation.

DL, then hit about .185 until June, when it was too late already."

"Okay, so I made a mistake. Stop *hocking* me, I'm as depressed as you are."

"God, depressed?"

"You're surprised?"

"Well, yes, I am."

"I don't know why you should be. The Torah says man was made in God's image, right? So why do you think you get depressed when the Cubs lose?"

"So that's the reason. Listen, people are asking me if you are still really a Cubs fan, after the way they've played this year."

"I don't know, sometimes I wonder why I give a good me-damn. I mean if I didn't have the Cubs to worry about, I could spend time on something else, like repairing the universe."

"That would be good."

"I was almost hoping for a strike. That would have been it, I'd have had it then."

"So, if you were hoping for a strike, why didn't you just cause one?"

"Well, I almost did, I toyed with it."

"What do you mean you toyed with it?"

"Well, I did the Pharoah thing, hardening the hearts of the owners and the players union."

"Why didn't that work?"

"Oh, it worked. I hardened their hearts all right. I just didn't make their brains stupid enough to forget their greed, so they settled."

"But you still haven't said whether you're giving up on the Cubs."

"I should, really. But they have some awfully good young pitching, y'know."

"Yes, but they're weak at other positions."

"But take a look at the talent they have coming up—Corey Patterson, Bobby Hill, Hee Seop Choi."

"Yes, but the other Cubs are getting old."

"Sure, but Sosa has a couple good years left. And Moises was hitting like hell for the last half of the season. He'll probably have a great year next year."

"And the relief pitching?"

"We can sign a free agent or two, or trade for some bullpen help."

"But what about the catching? You can't win without a good catcher."

"Maybe Hundley just had a couple bad years. 2003 could be the year he turns it all around."

"Wait a minute, you really think Hundley can turn it around? I am in awe of your faith. You *are* still a Cubs fan."

"Yeh, I guess so. Look, excuse me, but I gotta scoot, I'm only half way thorough inscribing people into the book of life."

"Okay, but do me a favor, please inscribe me in there. I want to be around when the Cubs win the World Series."

"Hah. I'm not even sure that I'm going to be around that long. *L'shanah tova*, see you at Opening Day."

2003

Five Outs Away

*Even after their middling 2002 campaign, the Cubs' personnel
changed little in the off-season – except to hire manager Dusty
Baker, who had just steered the San Francisco Giants to the World
Series. A toothpick-twiddling blues fan, Baker was hailed as an
inspired hire, though he would say in spring training, "I'm only as
good as they play."*

*The Cubs were playing .500 baseball before July's All-Star break
– a plain upgrade from the year before, but without much to distinguish the season other than Sammy Sosa's getting ejected for using
a corked bat against the Tampa Bay Devil Rays on June 3. It wasn't
until a July 23 trade with the Pittsburgh Pirates that brought a
young slugger named Aramis Ramirez (like Sosa, a Dominican)
to man third base, that Chicago found its identity. That trade also
imported journeymen Kenny Lofton and Randall Simon, who
two weeks earlier had casually bopped and toppled a woman in
an Italian sausage costume with his bat during the Milwaukee
Brewers' between-innings "sausage race." As a perennial league
strikeout leader, Simon confirmed his reputation as a player who
would swing at anything.*

But the Cubs had more than their bats working for them. Merely an average offensive team, they boasted perhaps the best starting pitching rotation anywhere, featuring a reassembled Kerry Wood, a Cy Young contender in Mark Prior, and a blossoming Carlos Zambrano. The Cubs went on a late-season tear, compiling a 33-20 record in August and September, on the way to winning their division for the first time since 1989. Wood and Prior finished first and second in the league in strikeouts.

A back-and-forth five-game National League Divisional Series win over the Atlanta Braves – in which Prior outdueled erstwhile Cubs pitcher Greg Maddux in a pivotal Game 3, and Ramirez whacked a two-run homer in the decisive Game 5 – gave the Cubs their first postseason series win in 95 years. Facing the upstart Florida Marlins for a berth in the Fall Classic, the Cubs took a 3-1 series lead. Needing one win in the final three games to advance to their first World Series since 1945, the Cubs proceeded to get shut out in Miami in Game 5. Back in Wrigley Field, they closed to within five outs of ending the series when a fan named Steve Bartman made an attempt at a foul ball that leftfielder Moises Alou was tracking. Alou responded to the minor setback by throwing a tantrum on the field, the blundering Cubs surrendered eight quick runs, and security escorted Bartman out of Wrigley a suddenly despised man.

That the poor fan was reflexively trying to make a catch on a foul ball – an act that almost anyone in Wrigley would have committed – didn't help him live down the undeserved infamy. By the time the Marlins shellacked Wood in Game 7, the conclusion felt foregone. Florida went on to thump the Yankees for the World

Series title. And on the North Side of Chicago, Bartman joined a
long list of scapegoats for a century of futility.

● ●

Fishing in the Desert

YESSSSSSSSSSSSSSSSSSSS.

This is my twentieth consecutive Open Mike, starting in 1984 with my ill-fated prediction that God would prove his existence to everyone beyond any doubt by ushering the Cubs into the World Series. Okay, so I jumped the gun a little bit.

As usual, this year I looked at the standings and found that a Chicago team had collapsed, dropping from a 2-game lead in their division on September 1 to six games behind on September 25. So I guess I should talk about the White Sox this year? I don't think so, *Bubbela.*

Religion is supposed to help us resolve our ethical dilemmas, but sometimes it creates them. Take this *Rosh Hashanah,* for example, I had the Cubs schedule set up perfectly. A 2:20 game on *Erev Rosh Hashanah,* plenty of time to get to services after the game, even if there are extra innings. And a 3:05 game on *Rosh Hashanah,* plenty of time to go to services before the game, even figuring in a very long sermon and 45 minutes of announcements.

So, what happens? The *Erev Rosh Hashanah* game gets rained out and they schedule a doubleheader starting at noon on *Rosh Hashanah.* Seeking to avoid the ethical dilemma, I get to services early on *Erev Rosh Hashanah* and tell our

Rabbi, "Look, we've gotta make a little adjustment tomorrow morning. We'll have to start services at 7 AM." Inexplicably, Brant refuses to go along with my plan. Well, fine by me; but there goes any contribution I might have made to the new building.

So, anyway, at *Rosh Hashanah* services, I'm davening pretty much prayer-by-prayer as to how long I'll stay, but I finally decide to stick it out through the sermon. I have to admit, though, I was tempted to take off right after the sermon began. Once I heard it was about war, I was pretty sure Brant was going to go out on a limb and come out against it. But I stayed, arriving at Wrigley in the bottom of the fourth, having missed three and a half innings of the first game because of my devout faith. Did I feel *frum*. And the Cubs win two.

Then, of course, comes last night, *Erev Yom Kippur*. As the cantor finishes *Kol Nidre*, the first pitch of the last game of the division series is thrown out. Never has the imagery of being written into the book of life or the book of death seemed so powerful to me. What to do? Well, I figured that if Hank Greenberg and Sandy Koufax could sit out games on *Yom Kippur*, I could go to *Kol Nidre* services (admittedly sitting at the back of the church/*shul* for a quick getaway, of course). And the Cubs win.

Is this the best High Holidays ever, or what?

I was remarkably calm for the final divisional game last night, for two reasons. First of all, I knew the Cubs would win. Though I'm not much on that numerology stuff, occasionally it becomes so overwhelming that one cannot resist believing. What do I mean? The two ace Cubs pitchers, Kerry Wood and Mark Prior, together have how many letters in their names? That's right, eighteen, *chai*, life. Okay, that could be an accident, but what about Farnsworth and Borowski together; again eighteen, *chai*. You're still skeptical? You are some tough cookies. Okay, get this, the three Pirates acquired by the Cubs—Randall Simon, Kenny Lofton and Aramis Ramirez? Together they have thirty-six letters, two *chai*.

The second reason I was calm is that even if the Cubs had lost, this season had already become a success three months ago, when I went to the World Series. You doubt that I went to the World Series in June? Well, I ask you where else could I have been? Was I not watching the Cubs play the Yankees in Wrigley Field? The last time that happened, I was minus four years old. And even more important, I watched the Cubs beat the Yankees, something they had never in history done.

At this point, I must interject a story about your rabbi. I called Brant to offer him a ticket to one of the Cubs-Yankees games, and he turned me down. It seems that the game was going to conflict with an AIDS in Africa benefit at JRC. I'm sure that makes you feel very proud of your rabbi, right? Wait a minute, are you really happy having a rabbi whose values are so fundamentally screwed up that he would make a decision like that? I mean, we're talking the Yankees here. Somebody else couldn't have done the benefit? What makes him think he's so essential? The *chutzpah.* If we were in California, I'd be petitioning for a rabbinical recall; and in California, that usually induces some charismatic Arnold to run for the vacancy[1].

But I digress.

As everyone knows, Thursday, July 9, was the turning point in the Cubs' season. On that date then Pirates' first baseman Randall Simon was booked for misdemeanor battery for hitting one of the Milwaukee Brewers' racing

---

[1] Reference is to Arnold Rachlis, JRC's first rabbi, and California governor, Arnold Schwarzenegger.

sausages with his bat during their sprint around the bases between the sixth and seventh innings of the game.

The AP reported, and I am not making this up, "Film of Wednesday night's race showed that when the group went past the Pirates' third-base dugout, Simon took a two-handed chop at the Italian sausage character—portrayed by a 20-year-old South Milwaukee woman—hitting her from behind and causing her to tumble to the ground. As she fell, a nearby sausage—the hot dog—went down as well."

Why, you ask, did Randall Simon do this? When questioned, Simon said that he had felled the sausage to avoid being suspended as Sammy Sosa had been. It turns out that Randall had misunderstood the reason for Sammy's suspension. He thought Sosa had been suspended for failure to take the pork out with his bat.[2]

Anyway, five weeks after the wiener-bashing incident, the Cubs acquired Randall Simon, and promptly moved from just over .500 to the Central Division Championship. To what should we attribute this?

I think that God was sending us a clear message. Most of us are content to be observers when we see wrong in the world, especially when it does not affect us directly; but not Randall Simon. When he looked from the dugout steps at the bratwurst, hot dog, Italian sausage, and Polish sausage, Randall said to himself, "Wait a minute, this is not right, these are all *trayf*; where's the Hebrew National kosher hot

---

[2] Sosa was suspended for using a corked bat.

dog?" Instead of waiting for others to act, Randall Simon, following the model of many righteous gentiles throughout history, took his bat and clobbered that sausage.

But, you ask, is this what we Jews are to do, react with violence when we see wrongs? Of course not. Is not the Torah filled with metaphors? As the Reconstructionist rabbis would tell us, this incident, properly understood, means that we all must search honestly for our inner *trayf,* the *trayf* within each of our lives and—when we find it, we must clobber the hell out of it, metaphorically speaking. Only in this way will we achieve our personal and collective Central Division Championship, and, eventually *Tikkun Olam,* the World Series.

You will recall that as the Israelites crossed the desert and approached the Promised Land, they sent out scouts who reported back to Moses that they saw giants. As the Cubs leave the desert and approach their Promised Land, our scouts thought they would see Giants, too; but instead they reported back to Moises that they saw fish, the Marlins.

When you see fish in the desert, it's definitely time for the Cubs to win a World Series. So watch as Randall Simon gets the Series-winning hit. *Hashanah Hazeh B'Wrigley Field.* This year in Wrigley Field.

2004

After the Crash

Before the 2004 season began, Kerry Wood remarked, "This is the first time since I've been a Cub where there's been talk of a World Series, as opposed to 'We're gonna have a good season, we're gonna get over .500.'" That goes a long way toward explaining how the Cubs could experience a second-straight winning season for the first time in more than 30 years, and still emerge so woefully disappointed as they did in 2004.

Expectations, for once, were soaring. The Cubbies famously had been five outs from advancing to the World Series, losing flukishly to a Florida team that beat the Yankees for the title and then, in true Marlins fashion, excommunicated all the (expensive) players who made that happen. With manager Dusty Baker returning, along with the supporting cast intact plus offseason additions such as pitchers Greg Maddux and LaTroy Hawkins and slugger Derrek Lee aboard, Chicago now looked to be the cream of the National League.

Sports Illustrated tried to get ahead of the pack by predicting a World Series title for the Cubs: "Not since Teddy Roosevelt's presidency have the Cubs played in two straight postseasons. They'll reach it again, but they're thinking bigger." The Illinois state legislature did its part, passing a resolution in the spring declaring that "the Cubs' curse shall be no more."

Somehow, even that foolproof approach didn't work. Sammy Sosa and Kerry Wood and Mark Prior all got hurt. As the ship took on water, general manager Jim Hendry made yet another deft move, acquiring All-Star shortstop Nomar Garciaparra from the Boston Red Sox in a four-team deal at the trade deadline.

Matters were never abysmal, but a 6–11 stretch in the spring and a 3-9 stretch in July did the Cubs no favors, even as Sosa became the team's all-time home run leader and Maddux became the 22nd pitcher in baseball history to win 300 games. A 2–7 skid to end the season dropped the Cubs from a 1 ½ game lead in the Wild Card to a merely respectable 89-73 record: good for third place in the stacked NL Central (and just the 16th winning season for the franchise since its last Series appearance, in 1945). They were three games behind the Houston Astros, who claimed the Wild Card spot – and a full 16 games behind the powerhouse St. Louis Cardinals, who defeated the Astros in the National League Championship Series for the right to suffer a Series sweep by, of all teams, the Red Sox.

Boston's Series win exorcised the Curse of the Bambino and thus made hash of almost 90 years of fatalistic Red Sox Nation gripes or answered an equivalent backlog of prayers, depending on how you viewed it. The Cubs wandered yet.

Backing Bartman

WE JEWS NEVER DWELL ON the past. (Okay, maybe we'll mention Egypt, occasionally.) So I hope you'll forgive me if I glance back briefly at events that occurred around last *Yom Kippur* at the Reconstructionist Yeshiva, Wrigley Field. Yes, the Yeshiva. I mean, it seems to me you either study Torah, or you go to Wrigley Field, right? Doing both would be redundant.

And where else are you going to go to study Torah, these days, anyway? Oh, sure, Torah study is theoretically available at JRC every Saturday morning. But, as you all know, that's not a realistic possibility, because it conflicts with *Car Talk* on NPR. When I pointed that out to Brant, he said that we could tape it. I said I thought that was a great idea, but he's yet to produce a single tape of the Torah study for me.

But I digress. Yes, Wrigley Yeshiva, where Torah comes to life. I mean if you want to know how Moses felt looking at the Promised Land from that mountain, what better parallel could you conjure than a lifelong Cubs fan watching the sixth game of the Marlins series at Wrigley last year, the Cubs leading 3 games to 2 and ahead 3–0 in the eighth inning with Mark Prior pitching? But, once again, Cubs fans were denied entry into the Promised Land. God set before us—as He says in the Torah—a blessing and a curse. The question we Jews might ask is, "Why do the Cubs always choose the curse?"

In this case, as in most cases, the answer can be found

right smack in the Talmud, which teaches us that a man should act *b'ratzon tov*, with great desire. *B'ratzon tov*—*b'rt*——of course, is an acronym for what? For Bart, as in Bartman, who acted just as he was instructed to act in the Talmud, and just as forty thousand other Yeshiva *bochers* would have done had they been in his seat, with great desire, to try to catch a foul ball.

So all of this public Bartman-loathing is anti-Semitism, pure and simple. And I say that we Jews have gotta put an end to it, once and for all. How? Simple; we stick up for Bartman the same way the multitude protected Spartacus in that famous scene from the 1960 movie. In fact, the congregation could even raise a little money, by selling t-shirts with the words, "I'm Bartman" on them. Just imagine 40,000 fans rising as one in their t-shirts, proclaiming, "I'm Bartman. I'm Bartman," creating a veritable wave of "I'm Bartmans." Oy, if Stanley Kubrick were only alive today.

I've gotta admit, though, this season has been a tough one.
I mean, look at that Cubs team on paper—and they may not
even make the playoffs. How can we explain that? [Sneeze]
Excuse me. By the way, Sammy Sosa does that in May—
sneezes—and he winds up on the DL, and misses 30 games.
And most of the rest of the team was on the disabled list for
a good part of the season, too. In the seventh inning, instead
of "Take Me Out to the Ball Game," we all should have been
singing Debbie Friedman's *Mi Sheberach*.[1] In fact, if I had
been the general manager of the Cubs, instead of trading
for an injured Nomar Garciaparra in August, I would have
traded for a trainer. Some nice Jewish doctor whose mother
could have made the team chicken soup, and the Cubs could
all have lived and been well, and gone to the World Series.

But even though, in Nomar, we didn't get somebody of
sound body, at least his replacement's very name embodies
soul. You know his replacement, Nefesh Perez. Well, what
did you think Nefei was short for?

Anyway, besides all the sickness we suffered through this
year, in August, all of a sudden, cement starts falling on us
from the upper deck of Wrigley Yeshiva. Remember, this is
a ballpark that has been in existence for 90 years. And we're
supposed to believe that this happens by accident, just like
that? Well I don't think so, *Bubbela*.

It's obvious that there can be only one explanation. The
Cubs troubles this season are the work of terrorists. I think

---

[1] A prayer for healing of the sick.

the falling cement in Wrigley is concrete evidence that those terrorists possess, and will not hesitate to use, Weapons of Lax Construction. But don't just take my word for that. In a speech last week aimed at attracting the critical Jewish Reconstructionist vote, Vice President Cheney suggested that, if John Kerry wins the election, terrorists will make sure that the Cubs go through another 96 years without winning a World Series.

Of course, Kerry countered by reminding voters that, when George Bush owned the Texas Rangers, he traded Sammy Sosa for Fred Manrique, who went on to slug a total of 20 home runs in his illustrious major league career. "Do we want somebody with that kind of judgment at the helm of our ship of state?" Kerry asked, rhetorically. "No," he answered, "I say, it's time to trade presidents."

But, soft, I'm in danger of violating our hallowed Open Mike rules against making political speeches. So I'm going to forego entirely my pro-Alan Keyes pitch.

In closing, I'd like to teach you all a new ending that I have composed to the Open Mike. If Bob Appelbaum can write all of that wonderful music for our services, I figure the least I can do is compose a closing for the Open Mike. Are you ready? This is in honor of both Garciaparra and Moises. So, as we conclude this year's Open Mike, please chant after me, "V'nomar Aloooooooo."[2]

---

[2] Hebrew would be, "And let us say, 'Alou.'"

2005

Sammy Who?

Mike Fontenot, Jerry Hairston, and Dave Crouthers together con-
stitute the answer to a trivia question that would stump even many
serious Cubs fans. That is, whom did the Baltimore Orioles trade to
the Cubs for Sammy Sosa?

Not exactly a murder's row in exchange for a surefire Hall of
Famer, but that's what the Cubs got (along with $10 million in
relief from Sosa's salary). Mostly the Cubs bought the relief of
parting ways with their aging, declining, fractious slugger. The
Orioles got the media circus that followed Sosa, who in March was
among several players called before Congress to testify on the use
of illegal steroids in baseball; and then they got 14 home runs and
a .221 average from the oft-injured outfielder. They finished fourth
in the American League East for the seventh time in eight seasons,
and didn't re-sign Sosa after the season.

Chicago, meanwhile, had enjoyed nine straight seasons with at
least 35 home runs and 100 RBI from Sosa, leaving natural questions about the Cubs' offense. Into that void stepped Derrek Lee.
A year after being acquired from the Marlins, having never batted

.300 over a full season, Lee hit .376 with National League-leading totals in RBIs, homers, runs, on-base percentage, total bases ... basically, everything that scores. He cooled by September and missed the Triple Crown, but his *.335 average still led the National League, making Lee the first Cub since Bill Buckner in 1980 to win a batting title.*

Other than Lee, though, the offense struggled, scoring only the 20th-most runs in the Majors. The pitching staff, which looked to be stellar with virtual dual aces in Mark Prior and Kerry Wood, was almost as mediocre while those two gentlemen dealt with injuries. Rick Morrissey summarized their plight in the Tribune in June: "The Cubs are looking forward to a long future with Prior and Wood. That's fine. It's the near future that's dicey." And it wasn't just the hurlers: Nomar Garciaparra, Todd Walker, and Aramis Ramirez all spent part of their summer vacations nursing injuries.

The Cubs' record was an even .500 at least once apiece in May, June, July and August – but that last one came during an eight-game losing streak that pushed the team into the red for the remainder of the season, as Chicago sank to fourth place in the NL Central. As for the trio the Cubs got for Sosa? Fontenot spent time in the minors before earning a spot as a back-up second baseman starting in the 2007 season; Hairston hit four home runs in 152 games with the Cubs in 2005 and 2006 before being traded; and Crouthers retired before the 2005 season to return to college, never playing a game for the Cubs.

The World Series went to the long-suffering White Sox, who swept the Houston Astros to bring the World Series crown to

Chicago for the first time since the last Sox win, way back in 1917.
The mantle of the second-longest World Series drought then passed
to the Cleveland Indians – who won their last title in 1948. A ways
back, but still a full 40 years since the Cubs' last such win.

Adding Injury to Insult

SOME SEASONS JUST ARE NOT funny.

In fact, I was going to pass on Open Mike until some guy wrote to me, after reading *Is God a Cubs Fan?*, and said, "Dear Arnie: I take pride in Chicago's reputation as a city of grit and character, and the Cubs' suffering has definitely contributed to that character; we clearly owe the team a debt of gratitude. Keep writing." So, okay Barack Obama, this Yom Kippur's for you.

I'm happy to report that there's strong evidence that the relationship between God and the Cubs is finally being recognized by other religions. For example, at Ryne Sandberg's induction into the Hall of Fame in Cooperstown this summer, Robert Corral, a Franciscan friar, concluded his invocation with, "Dear God, could you please, please, please remember the Cubs this year?" Apparently, though, Friar Robert's plea slipped the mind of The Omnipotent One.

Along with Sandberg, former Boston Red Sox great, Wade Boggs, was inducted into the Hall of Fame. No, Boggs is not Jewish, but before each of his at-bats Wade used to draw the Hebrew symbol for *chai* with his foot in the batter's box dirt.

I am not making this up. Maybe we should see if we could teach Corey Patterson how to do that.

By the way, I don't think that trading Corey is the answer. First of all, as soon as the Cubs trade Corey, he'll become the next Lou Brock. And trading him would not remove the Patterson curse, anyway. The Cubs minor league player of the year this year was a second baseman with their double-A farm team, the West Tennessee JAXX; Eric Patterson. Yup, you guessed it, Corey's younger brother. But I digress.

Now some people attribute the Cubs' lousy performance this year to their tough luck with injuries. At various times during the season:

Kerry Wood

Mark Prior

Aramis Ramirez

Nomar Garciaparra

Todd Walker

Jerry Hairston

Mike Remlinger

Chad Fox

and Scott Williamson

were on the disabled list.

All of those injuries might even have caused some of you to question whether God has abandoned the Cubs altogether. The answer to that is a resounding, "No." And I'll tell you why.

As you know, we Reconstructionists rejected the notion that Jews are the Chosen People when we changed *asher bahar banu* to *asher kervanu* in the Torah blessing. And I understand why that's a politically wise position to take. We certainly don't want to come across to people of other faiths as claiming we're the one true religion, at least not publicly. But, hey c'mon, we're all *mishpocha* here. And we are like so totally chosen.

But what's Chosenness got to do with the Cubs, you ask? I'm glad you asked.

This year God sent one of his Chosen to the Cubs. (I'm not saying it was his only son, but it was definitely one of the kids). On July 9, Adam Greenberg made his first major league appearance, pinch hitting for Cubs' pitcher Will Ohman in the Cubs–Marlins game down in Miami. In the stands were his parents, Wendy and Mark, his brothers Max and Sam and his sister, Loren, all of whom had flown down from Connecticut for the game. (Evidently Adam's Uncle Hershel, Uncle Morris, Aunt Edith, Aunt Mildred and cousins Ashley, Tiffany, Wyatt, and Cooper couldn't make it). Anyway, on the very first pitch thrown to him, Adam was hit in the back of the head and was helped off the field, as the stands erupted as one in a mighty *"Oy vey!"*

Though Adam did not make it back up to the Cubs this season, fortunately he has recovered completely. In fact, as we speak, Adam is *davening* down in Venezuela, where he is playing winter ball before he reports to the Cubs for Spring Training. So next year is definitely the Cubs year, and it will be a Jew who makes it all happen. Why do I say this with such complete confidence?

Well, students of the game of baseball know that one of the most critical statistics for a team's offense is their batters' on-base percentage. An on-base percentage of .400 is considered outstanding. Having been hit by a pitch and awarded first base in his only at-bat, Adam Greenberg is the only major league player—dead or alive—with an on-base percentage of 1,000.

So, just imagine the Cubs next year with a Jewish player who gets on base every time he comes to bat. Now if that doesn't put the *asher baher banu* back into the Torah blessing I don't know what will.

*L'shannah ha ba-a b'*Wrigley Field.

2006

Everybody Hurts

For a while there, the Cubs looked decent. They were 9-5 on April 21 when the Dodgers' Rafael Furcal collided with Derrek Lee at first base, breaking the wrist of the Cubs' top slugger. The team held steady, actually reaching a 13-8 record ... then won just 53 of the final 141 games, winding up with the worst record in the National League, and, at 66 wins, the worst for the Cubs since 2000.

Lee's fluke injury was, it turned out, just the first among several. Pitcher Glendon Rusch developed blood clots in his lungs that kept him from starting more than nine games. Injuries again made Kerry Wood and Mark Prior near-nonentities: When Wood, he of the 20 strikeouts in a single game, only strikes out 13 batters during the course of the season, it's fair to say Chicago is hurting. The Cubs traded the struggling Greg Maddux to the Dodgers at the end of July. Only righthander Carlos Zambrano thrived. In addition to slugging six home runs, a record for a pitcher, Zambrano compiled a 3.41 ERA that pushed him to a fifth-place finish in the

Cy Young Award voting, and his 16 wins against 9 losses made him the only Cubs pitcher with a winning record.

Lee was out, then returned with pain, then was out, and was activated late in the season, hitting a grand slam on Sept. 6, his 31st birthday (his fourth straight birthday with a homer). In his absence, the Cubs could hit for average but had no power. Their opponents hit 125 homers at Wrigley Field; the Cubs, just 81. Their best run producer, Aramis Ramirez, didn't really get clicking until the second half of the season. By then, the Cubs were buried.

At season's end, Cubs president and CEO Andy MacPhail bowed out after 12 years on the job. "This is the first thing I've ever done in baseball," he explained at a news conference, "that I didn't have a high level of success at." After designing the Minnesota Twins teams that won two World Series titles, he had just two post-season appearances with the Cubs.

Dusty Baker was the next to hit the bricks, after four seasons at the helm. Though they considered former Cubs pitcher Joe Girardi, the Cubs hired veteran manager Lou Piniella, perhaps the anti-Dusty, best known for turning around a sad-sack franchise in Seattle and for speaking his mind to umpires. Shortly after the St. Louis Cardinals thumped the Detroit Tigers to win the World Series, the Cubs committed a trainload of money to the likes of Ramirez, pitcher Ted Lilly, Mark DeRosa, Jason Marquis, and outfielder Alfonso Soriano, whom the Cubs landed for a mere $136 million, the fifth-largest deal in baseball history. If they overpaid, at least the Cubs' front office committed to righting the flailing franchise.

Unaligned Planets

AS THE *CHACHAM* REB AVRAHAM of Mudville was fond of saying, "Well, you can't win 'em all."

Sure we finished last, thirty games under .500. But if you think this was a tough season for Cubs fans, our pain is nothing compared to the disappointment suffered by others this year.

Take Pluto, for instance. Imagine thinking that you're a planet for more than 75 years, rotating patiently around the sun, even though it takes you 248 years to do it, and then waking up one day to be told that you're a damn asteroid, a dwarf planet. I mean, so big deal if your orbit happens to go inside Neptune's; it would kill Neptune to move over a little? Of all the planets, Pluto was clearly the Jewish grandmother planet; the only planet that had not been visited by a spacecraft. Not so much as a postcard. And now it's too late; Bubbe is gone. But I digress.

Actually, as true Cubs fans know, this was a great season. Oh, sure, it would be easy enough to dwell upon little disappointments. Allowing a runner to score from second base on a sacrifice fly. Permitting two runners to score on a ground ball to the shortstop. Your star third baseman getting hit in the head with a foul pop fly. Making six errors in a game. Losing when your ace reliever walks two men and throws two wild pitches in a third of an inning.

But we need to look at the bigger picture. Most years, we Cubs fans are suffering through the summer and early fall, wondering whether we're going to make the playoffs. This year, by Flag Day, we were like totally chilled. And the Cubs are now in a perfect position to become the club with the most improved record in 2007.

Many fans point to Michael Barrett as one of the few bright spots in the Cubs' season. They rejoice in the fact that he slugged the White Sox catcher, A.J. Pierzynski, in the jaw on May 20, when Pierzynski was not looking. A hot-selling t-shirt outside of Wrigley Field shows a picture of the punch with a caption of "Who says the Cubs can't hit?" Of course, the Cubs lost the game, 7–0, but nobody notices that. And Barrett was suspended for ten games, after trying to excuse or mitigate what he did by giving almost as many versions of what happened as our President has given reasons for the war in Iraq.

Personally, I have a tough time working up any sympathy for Barrett, and I don't find what he did entertaining. I go to Wrigley Field to see baseball. If I were interested in seeing guys punched in the jaw, I'd go to a hockey game. So I figured that, if there were any divine justice, Barrett's stats would nose dive after he returned from his suspension.

In fact, though, the opposite occurred. He started hitting even better. Now I suppose you could argue that he was punished enough because the ten games he missed cost him over $250,000 in salary. But when you're making more than $4,300,000 a year, you hardly notice that.

So, I was pondering the implications of all of this for the question of whether God was a just God at the Cubs–Giants game on September 2, when Barrett was hit in the groin with a foul tip, and incurred an intrascrotal hemotoma. Ooh, just saying that—intrascrotal hemotoma—is painful. Now I know that that is not funny, and I take no pleasure in the pain of others. But just think about how hard it is for a catcher to get hit in the crotch with a foul ball. I mean you're squatting there, with all that equipment on and you've got your glove right in front of you. Only a true Cub could do it. And surely, for it to happen, there must have been some higher power at work. Fortunately, Barrett is okay and, though he was unable to return to the Cubs this season, he is currently singing the mezzo role in Lyric Opera's production of *Turandot.*

But how to end this? As most of you probably know, there's an unwritten, but strictly-enforced, rule of Open Mikes, that no talk can end with a crotch story.

So I think that we must end where we began, with Pluto. It's pretty clear that the Cubs are the Pluto of the major leagues, a kind of dwarf team. So, if we imagine winning the World Series as the sun, then if the Cubs follow Pluto's elliptical orbit, we have only 150 more years to complete that orbit and win the World Series. So take heart, Cubs fans, the end is in sight. Just keep your eyes heavenward, and use a very powerful telescope.

L' Shana Ha Ba-a B' Milky Way.

2007

Fight to the Finish

*In his first spring as the Cubs manager, Lou Piniella made it clear
he didn't believe in curses. He went so far as to stomp on a stuffed
toy animal—a billy goat stand-in—and say, ''No curse!'' while
being filmed by a Japanese television crew. By season's end, the
Cubs would see no shortage of cursing, if not the alleged Billy Goat
Curse itself, but would, under Pinella's stewardship, make the
improbable leap from the worst record in the National League to
winning the NL Central.*

*They sure took their sweet time turning things around, though.
With a roster laden with expensive new talent, the Cubs expected a
record better than 22–29 after two months. "We're going through
a stretch right now where we're not scoring many runs," third
baseman Aramis Ramirez said after a late-May loss to the Florida
Marlins, whose payroll was less than a third of the Cubs'. "That's
not our only problem. We're not pitching and we're not hitting."
Piniella, likewise vexed, employed 42 different hitting lineups in
those first 51 games. To straighten out the clubhouse, Derrek Lee*

called a players-only meeting before a Wednesday game the Cubs subsequently lost.

Then something snapped. That Friday, in the middle of a particularly sloppy loss to the Atlanta Braves, pitcher Carlos Zambrano tussled with catcher Michael Barrett in the dugout, then again in the clubhouse. Barrett went to the hospital with a cut lip. (The pitcher-catcher fight led to a delicious headline pun: "aggravated battery.") The next day, Piniella argued a third base call forcefully enough to get tossed, then suspended for four games by Major League Baseball for making contact with the ump. Soon after, Barrett got in another squabble with another pitcher, and the Cubs shipped him to the San Diego Padres.

But in the first 24 games after Piniella's ejection, the Cubs won 16. And by the All-Star break, they'd clawed their way back to a half-game above .500, just 4.5 games behind the division-leading Milwaukee Brewers. Three weeks after that, the Cubs caught up. Even as they stumbled in August, so did Milwaukee; the Cubs clinched the division on Sept. 28, with just two games remaining. He dismissed any claim of cause-and-effect, but after Piniella's ejection, the Cubs finished on a 63–46 tear.

Forget that they had only the 12th-best record in baseball: the Cubs were back in the postseason, facing down the upstart Arizona Diamondbacks. Infamously, in Game 1, Piniella gave Zambrano the hook in the sixth inning, ostensibly to keep his pitch count low and rest the overworked ace for a potential Game 4. But when the normally reliable Carlos Marmol stepped in and served up a home run, breaking the 1–1 tie, the Diamondbacks claimed the first victory, behind their ace, Brandon Webb. Arizona won Game 2 in the desert, then finished the three-game sweep at Wrigley Field as the Cubs' big bats—e.g., 0-for-12 Aramis Ramirez—disappeared in the series, stranding nine runners on base in each game. "Well, Chicago Cubs, look at the bright side," columnist Gene Wojciechowski eulogized. "At least Carlos Zambrano will be totally rested for the season opener March 31."

Meanwhile, the Red Sox won another World Series title, sweeping a Colorado Rockies club that had played the previous month as if possessed by the 1927 Yankees. If there ever had been such a thing as the Curse of the Bambino, it, at least, was long gone.

• •

The Promised Land

THIS HAS BEEN A MOMENTOUS year for baseball and for Jews. After 5767 years, professional baseball finally reached the Promised Land, in the form of the IBL, the Israel Baseball League. Not that we haven't had a few Jewish stars in the Major Leagues over the years, but at last we have a baseball homeland, a place where Jewish ballplayers will prosper and stand out.

The first season is now over, and the IBL has announced its 2007 awards. In case you missed them, the co-winners of the Hank Greenberg award for the most valuable player were Eladio Rodriguez and Gregg Raymundo. And the award for the best pitcher in the IBL went to Juan Feliciano. But I don't want anyone to think that Jews did not distinguish themselves, because they did. Aaron Pribble and Brendan Rubenstein won the Commissioner's Award for

Sportsmanship and Character. I am not making any of this up.

Anyway, the Bet Shemesh Blue Sox won the first IBL title, shutting out the Modi'in Miracle, 3–0, in the championship game. So I think that it's about time for JRC to adopt an IBL team. And, it's clear to me who that team should be—the Petach Tikva Pioneers, who were managed until the last two weeks of the season by the winningest Jewish pitcher of all time, ex-Cub Kenny Holtzman. It's true that the Pioneers, had sort of a rough first season, finishing 9–32, which left them 20 games out of first, in a 41-game season. But just think of the possibilities our Pioneers will have for improvement next season.

We even have a local hero to root for on the Pioneers, Aaron Rosdal, an outfielder who resides in Chicago. According to the team website, Aaron's superstition is "I need to dance the hora before each game or else I won't play." I'm thinking that maybe the hora took a bit too much out of Aaron, because he wound up hitting .175 this season. On the other hand, only nine players on the Pioneers had a higher batting average. And I'm virtually certain that Aaron was a strong contender for the Commissioner's Sportsmanship and Character award.

But I digress. What about the Cubs? Well, management certainly did not skimp on the cash. Counting the recent signing of Carlos Zambrano—you know, the guy who doesn't like to be booed just because he is paid $91.5 million, punches his own catcher in the face and didn't win a game in over a month—the Cubs committed about $400 million this year. Personally, I think they could have used that money better. I mean, I did some math. The Cubs draw about 40,000 people a game. If they spread the $400 million evenly, that would be $10,000 per fan. Talk about a way of building fan loyalty. Hell, I'd even agree not to boo Carlos Zambrano; or any other Cub, for that matter.

I'm happy to report, that the Jews did get part of the $400 million the Cubs spent, Jason Marquis' contract for $21 million over three years. And there's some Talmudic numerology afloat in that $21 million figure, too. Marquis wears the number 21, which is the same number 21 that was worn by Sammy Sosa, to whom Marquis dished up his 600th home run. If Jason turns out to be a star, I'm planning to change the name of our standard poodle from Sosa to Marquis. I've always wanted a Jewish poodle who wore the number twenty-one for the Cubs.

The newspapers reported that Lou Piniella changed his pitching rotation for the last two weeks of the season to give his best pitchers another start. But Lou confided to me that the real reason he did it was so that Jason Marquis would not have to decide whether to pitch on Yom Kippur. I've wrestled with whether it would have been okay for Marquis to pitch today. In fact, during the silent Amidah this morning, I had a little chat with God about it. "Compassionate One," I asked, "would it have been okay for Marquis to pitch on Yom Kippur, even though Sandy Koufax refused to?"

"Hey, Boychick," the All-Knowing One replied, "maybe you haven't noticed, but Jason Marquis is no Sandy Koufax."

"I take your point, Sarcastic One, but would it have been okay?"

And the Merciful One replied, "If a Jew may eat on Yom Kippur to preserve his health and work on Shabbat to save a life, may not a Jewish Cubs pitcher in the heat of a pennant race pitch on Yom Kippur?"

Anyway, if the Cubs fail to win the World Series again, I think we ought to transfer them to the Israel Baseball League next season. We already have the baseball cap.

The Cubs may need to make some adjustments in the IBL. For example, I'm not sure whether, under Israeli rules, when you hit the ball you run to third base first. But that shouldn't adversely impact the Cubs base running. Any team that has a guy thrown out at the plate, running through the third base coach's stop signal with nobody out, and another runner who gets thrown out going from first base to second base when the batter walked, is liable to start running directly to third base soon, anyway.

Joining the IBL may be the best hope the Cubs have for ending their 100-year championship drought. And, then, next year we finally can say *L'shannah ha Ba-a B'Yerushalaim,* and be talking baseball.

2008

The Fall: Classic

*This was the season in which the words "first" and "since" kept
replaying, and for once, in a good way. The Cubs accumulated 97
wins for the first time since 1945, the year of their last World Series
appearance. At the All-Star break the Cubs shared the best record
in the Major Leagues with the Los Angeles Angels of Anaheim. The
eight players they sent to the Midseason Classic tied a National
League record. On April 23 the Cubs became the second Major
League franchise, after the Giants, to win 10,000 games. Just off
rehab from a shoulder injury, Carlos Zambrano mowed down the
Houston Astros on Sept. 14 for the Cubs' first no-hitter since 1972.*

*What propelled them? For starters, the starters: Ryan Dempster
(who won his first 10 starts at Wrigley Field), Ted Lilly, the
tempestuous Zambrano. The bats, too, included many of the
same cast who won the National League Central a season earlier:
Alfonso Soriano, Aramis Ramirez, Derrek Lee. Kerry Wood closed.
Further, the team added a brilliant rookie reliever in Jeff Samardzija
and a hungry young catcher, Geovany Soto, who hit 23 home
runs and won the NL Rookie of the Year award. A couple of solid*

veterans joined, as well: the ghost of ex-Cardinals center fielder Jim Edmonds, who rediscovered his bat; and Kosuke Fukudome, the first Japanese player to suit up for the Cubs, started hot but wilted during the course of the season.

The team's payroll was a robust $117 million, eighth-highest in the Majors. It led the NL in both runs scored and batting average against. It was a solid team, and far from a merely sentimental pick to advance deep into October, Chicago, which clinched its division on September 20, had the resolute look of a champion.

The Cubs advanced to a second consecutive postseason for the first time since 1906-08. Then, for the first time since 2007, the Cubs suffered a baffling collapse. Against the Joe Torre-managed Los Angeles Dodgers, Ryan Dempster, who had been almost unbeatable at Wrigley Field, struggled to throw strikes in losing Game 1, walking seven and serving up a grand slam in less than five innings. Each of Chicago's infielders committed an error in a 10-3 Game 2 loss, and the Cubs scored only a single run on eight hits in L.A. in Game 3. Two seasons under Piniella had brought two straight playoff sweeps. "Let me tell you this: You can play postseason baseball for now to another hundred years," he said afterwards, "but if you score six runs in three games, it's going to be another hundred years before we win."

It's hard to overstate how breathtaking the Cubs' postseason meltdown was, after the marvelous season they had built.

Chicago's consolation came when politics soon usurped sport. Six days after the long-suffering Philadelphia Phillies topped the long-suffering Tampa Bay Rays to win the Series, Chicago's own Barack Obama was elected the 44th President, and more than

100,000 revelers mobbed downtown Grant Park. The occasion prompted some to ponder whether, in 1908, it would have seemed fathomable that America would elect an African-American president before the Cubs won another World Series. Or whether a reasonable fan would have guessed the Cubs would go 100 full years without winning the championship. But then, as Cubs fans are fond of saying, anyone can have an off century.

. . . .

Apocalypse No

HELLO AGAIN.

Y'know, I really shouldn't be here. Since my personal reflection on *Rosh Hashanah,* my agent no longer permits me to talk to audiences this small. But, for you, I'm making an exception; just this once.

In 1984, I went with my heart in predicting that the Cubs would reach the World Series, thereby proving the existence of God. So much for the heart. This year, I opted for a more rational assessment. I decided to try the mind.

I asked myself, "Arnold, how can we determine whether the time is right?" Well, I reasoned, the Cubs winning the World Series would be an apocalyptic event. So we had to ask whether there were signs that the universe was preparing for such an apocalypse. I identified nine clear signs.

And, yet, we all know what happened. So, I was pretty puzzled. And I decided to ask God where I had gone wrong. Now I know that we Reconstuctionists are supposed to believe that God is that force within the universe that makes for good, or something like that. To that my reaction is, "C'mon, give me a break." So I have reconstructed the notion that God is a force for good within the universe to mean that God is some little old white dude with a long white beard and robe, sitting up in the sky.

So, I asked unto him, "All-Knowing Little Old White Dude with a Long White Beard and Robe, Sitting Up in the Sky, would it not be an apocalyptic event if the Cubs won the World Series?"

To which He replied, "Duh."

"And have there in fact not been many signs of such an apocalypse this year:

"First, the entire financial structure of the world has collapsed.

"Second, the candidates for president and vice president of the United States include a Black man and a white female moose hunter.

"Third, this season marks one hundred years—one century—since the Cubs last won the World Series.

"Fourth, this is the year that Yankee Stadium—the House that Ruth Built—is being destroyed. Better still, even before the physical destruction of the stadium, the Yankees themselves—the players that Steinbrenner bought—self-destructed.

"Fifth, this is the year in which the Cubs acquired their first Japanese ball player, Kosuke Fukodome. And the Japanese alphabet is like totally inscrutable. So that's something.

"Sixth, each year at the JRC benefit, I auction off tickets for
a Cubs game with me and the rabbi. This year's game was
against the Astros on Monday, August 4, the night, you will
recall, on which you flung down 90,000 bolts of lightning and
caused a Biblical deluge to descend upon Wrigley Field. As
Brant, the Davidsons and I boarded the el home, we noticed
that you had reserved one car that looked to be roughly 40
cubits high for a pair of male and female ball players who
play each position. (And, of course, we should not fail to note
that the word 'cubit' contains the word 'Cub' within it and, in
fact, in ancient times, was pronounced 'Cub hit.' But I digress.)

"Seventh, again the Astros. When you smote Houston with Hurricane Ike, two of the games the Cubs were to have played there were moved to Milwaukee. Then did you bless Big Z with a no-hitter in the first game and curse the Astros, who had won 14 of their previous 15 games, allowing them a total of one hit in losing two games to the Cubs.

"Eighth, on the night of August 28, the 45th anniversary of Martin Luther King's "I Have a Dream" speech, as Barack Obama accepted the Democratic Party's nomination for president of the United States, in a stadium full of wildly cheering fans, Aramis Ramirez socked a grand slam home run in the last of the eighth to lead the Cubs to an improbable 6–4 win over the Phillies at Wrigley Field. Same principle; different dreams.

"And finally, ninth, one year ago, I planned a trip to Africa. Carol and I leave tomorrow and will be gone for the World Series. This was to be my sacrifice, so that other Cubs fans should live and be happy."

Whereupon, the Little Old White Dude spake unto me, saying, "Verily, what you say is true. All of these matters you have enumerated are signs of an impending apocalypse."

"Then, Dude, like where did I go wrong?" I asked.

And He replied, "In the torah, it is said, 'Lo b'shamayim.' It is not in the heavens or beyond the seas—or in the sky boxes—that answers reside, but rather very near to you. In other words, Boychick, 'Apocalypse, acropolis; those bums lost three straight games to the damn Dodgers. Are these, by you, world champions?'"

So, in the end, all of those signs around Wrigley Field this season predicting, "It's Gonna Happen" were prophetic. They needed only add, "Again."

But, not to worry, the 2009 season starts a brand new century for the Cubs, and I have a feeling that this just might be our century. Right, Dude?

NO SILVER ANNIVERSARY LINING

Night games, on-field advertising and $45 bleacher seats. Other than that, not much has changed for Wrigley Field and the Cubs in the past quarter-century.

Twenty-five is a number both round and square. Ditto 100, the number of years, and counting, the Cubs have waited for a title. They seem like eons, but in Cubs Nation, 25 years is a blip. A down payment. It wasn't for nothing that Cubs fans made "wait 'til next century" a rallying cry.

Baseball has done nothing but chug along in that span, through strike and steroids scandals and expansion. The average salary of a major league player has increased tenfold to more than $3 million a year; total annual attendance has gone from 45 million to 73 million. Since that teeth-gnashing 1984 season—in which the Cubs' hearts were broken by the San Diego Padres, of all teams— 23 different teams have gone to the World Series (including three teams that didn't exist in 1984) and 17 different teams have won it.

Meanwhile, at Wrigley, history plays hooky with an Old Style in one hand and a brat in the other. Consider: You can trace virtually the entirety of the Cubs' past 25 years through just three players, Ryne Sandberg, Mark Grace, and Kerry Wood.

Known for his major league record fielding percentage for a second baseman, Ryno was a rare slugging infielder before those became the highest-paid players in the sport. He turned 25 during his brilliant Most Valuable Player 1984 season. He welcomed

Andre Dawson, the next Cubs MVP, three years later. He was there the night in '88 when the Cubs caught up to the 1940s and played at Wrigley at night.

That was the year, too, he started throwing to a rookie first baseman named Mark Grace. When the Cubs made the playoffs again in 1989, it was Grace who nearly willed them to the World Series. He was a Cub through some truly forgettable seasons, including the strike-shortened debacle that was 1994. When Sammy Sosa's moonshots left the country agog, and led the Cubs back to the playoffs in 1998, he was batting cleanup behind Grace, who collected the most hits of any major leaguer during the 1990s.

A rookie in 1998, Wood tied a record with 20 strikeouts in just his fifth start. He became the fastest player in baseball history to record 1,000 career strikeouts, nearly aced the Cubs to a World Series berth in 2003, fought through injury after injury, gamely accepted a closer's roll, and after a workmanlike 2008 season— which marked the first time in a century that the Cubs advanced to the playoffs a second straight time—was told his services were no longer needed.

As with Sandberg and Grace, the Cubs won't be the same without Wood. And yet, they will.

ON FURTHER REFLECTION

Besides the open mike tradition at JRC, there is a custom of asking two members of the congregation to offer a personal reflection during the course of the High Holiday services, one on Rosh Hashanah and one on Yom Kippur. The following remarks, celebrating 25 years of Cubs Open Mikes, were delivered on the first day of Rosh Hashanah morning, 2008.

HAVING TOILED FOR THE PAST 24 years in the obscurity of Open Mike Land, where one is limited, in theory, to three minutes, I can't tell you what a thrill it is to be here. Sitting in the pews on the *bimah* on *Yom Kippur* afternoon, dreaming of a corned beef sandwich on rye, with a pickle, which of us Open Mikers has not thought, as we awaited our turn, "Man, if I only had a crack at a personal reflection."

And then, one day, that phone rings and Bryna, on the other end, says, "Pack your Hebrew Cubs hat, Kanter, you're on your way to the Bigs."

Soon thereafter, though, reality sets in, and the demons of self-doubt dance, like sugar plum designated hitters, in your head. Does baseball, and the Cubs in particular, belong center-stage in a High Holiday service? What does our national pastime have to do with the lessons of religion?

And, worse still, as I began to reflect on my reflection, it occurred to me, sadly, that just maybe there's something slightly sick about a 65-year old guy caring about whether the Cubs win or lose.

So, in the hour and a half I plan to talk today, I want to muse on why caring about baseball and the Cubs, for me, fits hand-in-glove with our religion.

Let's start with the importance of place. Whether in the presence of the Ark of the Covenant, as it wended its way through the desert—which, unfortunately, I missed out on—or at the Wailing Wall in *Eretz Yisrael*—at which I've yet to wail—whether in the cramped quarters of the old JRC; our temporary, HVAC-challenged building; the beautiful new JRC structure with its Wrigley Field-inspired ivy walls; or in this, our High Holidays church—can any of us imagine celebrating the High Holidays in a synagogue?—place matters. Place instills a sense of holiness. And, for me, it is impossible to sit out at Wrigley Field on a beautiful, sunny afternoon (or even on a breezy evening) and not experience a sense of the divine.

The value of tradition. In Judaism, we eat the maror and drink four cups of wine, we wear a *kippah* and we sing *"shehehianu"* and *"dayenu."* In Cubsism, I eat kosher hot dogs and drink four Bud Lites (but not after the seventh inning), which I purchase from my regular beer vendor, Bob Chicoine (who, by the way, is also an accomplished poet), I wear a Hebrew Cubs hat and I sing "Take Me Out to the Ball Game" and "Hey, Chicago, What Do You Say, the Cubs Are Going to Win Today." So, not a whole lot of difference there.

Success is not perfection. On *Yom Kippur* we repent,

confess that we have not done all that we might have, confident that we may still be written into the Book of Life. Baseball makes this point even more clearly. When I get frustrated, on the rare occasions on which I'm unable to achieve perfection, I remember that, if I'd had a bit more baseball talent, hitting safely just three out of ten times might have written me into the Hall of Fame, where I could have *davened* with Sandy Koufax and Hank Greenberg.

Everyone makes a difference. At JRC, we have folks who serve on the Board or on committees, provide food for onegs, volunteer at soup kitchens, chant torah, donate money or clothes, usher for the High Holidays, and sing in the choir. Without them, JRC would not be JRC. The Cubs have coaches, trainers, clubhouse attendants, and players who hit home runs, who pitch the seventh inning, who steal a base, who bunt a runner into scoring position, who make a terrific fielding play, who pinch hit or pinch run, and who fill in at several positions. Without them, the Cubs would not be the Cubs.

The power of community. All of us at JRC recognize the central role of community to our congregation. Whether it's the pleasure of greeting people you know at services, praying or working together, or helping out or being helped in a time of difficulty, we value community. Singing "Take Me Out to the Ball Game" during the seventh inning, jumping up to cheer a home run, or high-fiving an absolute stranger after a Cubs win creates for me some of that same sense of community at Wrigley Field.

Cultivating wonder. At its best, religion helps us to appreciate some of the simple things we take for granted, from the wonders of nature—I love to look out at the trees through the windows of our new sanctuary—to the kindness of fellow congregants. The older I get, it's not the home runs that I love best in baseball (though, don't get me wrong, I like those plenty well), but the seemingly routine play made by a shortstop who runs far to his right, backhands the ball, and, in the same motion, throws to first to nip the runner. Though this play won't show up in the box score, may hardly be noticed, it is a supremely athletic, beautiful and basically impossible feat. The same might be said of a batter simply managing to hit a ball thrown at 97 miles an hour. Baseball has helped me learn to marvel at the routine.

Stuff happens. Life does not always go smoothly. When it doesn't, that's often difficult to abide. Religion tries to give us some perspective on this. Over the course of a Cubs season, I can count on the fact that a relief pitcher will walk in the winning run, the Cubs will fail to score in a critical situation with the bases loaded and nobody out, an outfielder will cost them a game by dropping a routine fly ball, a runner representing the winning run will be picked off of third base, an opposing pitcher with an 8.00 ERA will strike out twelve Cubs and hold them scoreless, and an opposing batter with a .140 average will hit three home runs and drive in eight runs. Now you have two choices in those situations. You can aggravate the hell out of yourself, swear, and cause your blood pressure to soar. That's what I do. Or, as I hope someday to be able to do, when and if I mature, you can tell yourself, "Well, Arnold, that's too bad, but, y'know, stuff happens."

The value of sacrifice. Maimonides, I think, or Rashi, or maybe Moses said something about the levels of charity. Actually, it could have been Arnie Rachlis. Anyway, I know that you all remember this, which is good, because I don't, except that I know that the highest level had something to do with giving anonymously, without recognition. JRC recognized this hierarchy in a rather amazing way, by choosing to raise money for our new building without the traditional naming rights associated with making a large gift. This was actually quite courageous—and more than a bit disappointing to me, as I was really looking forward to establishing the Arnie Kanter Open Mike. Still, I can see how some might object to the Frito-Lay *Erev Rosh Hashanah* Service.

Baseball has its own levels of sacrifice. The sacrifice fly is good, but it's not that much of a sacrifice because it gives the batter an RBI. The sacrifice bunt allows the batter to avoid an at-bat. But the highest form of sacrifice is the batter who, with a runner on second and no outs, punches a ground ball to the right side of the infield, putting the runner in position to score on a sacrifice fly, even though the batter is charged with making an out. Now that's giving anonymously.

Finding something outside ourselves. When we get bogged down in our own *mishagas*, Judaism teaches us the duty of *Tikkun Olam*, the healing of the world, of thinking of something larger than us. Baseball, on the other hand, has the virtue of focusing me on something smaller than myself. But at least it gets me to focus outside of myself, takes me away—temporarily—from the seemingly insolvable problems that we face as individuals or nations. Many of us need this escape badly. At least I do.

And speaking of the problems our nation faces, it would not be right, in this election year, to fail to point out the intersection between religion, God, and politics and how *Is God a Cubs Fan?* did what the Democratic Party was almost incapable of doing itself. For a long time, this book seemed to be the only thing on which Hillary Clinton and Barack Obama could agree.

In 2000, Senator Clinton wrote to me, "[Whether God is a Cubs fan] is a theological question I have asked myself many times and I am glad that you chose to devote your amusing little book to a problem that has perplexed me from girlhood. It might give you some comfort to know that Methodists all over the North Side have been asking the same question for years."

And in 2004, then-candidate for senator, Barack Obama— in a letter widely credited with having secured the Jewish vote for him—wrote, "Thanks for the book. Cub-mania is at a fever-pitch. I take pride in Chicago's reputation as a city of grit and character, and the Cubs' suffering has definitely contributed to that character; we clearly owe the team a debt of gratitude. Keep writing."

By the way, we don't know what Senator McCain thinks about *Is God a Cubs Fan?* We sent him a copy, but have not heard back from him. Maybe we sent it to the wrong house.

But I digress. . . .

There are many more parallels that I could draw between the lessons I have learned from both baseball and religion— the power of faith, the value of hard work, the virtue of loyalty, the ability to succeed against all odds, the tendency of things to balance out in the end, the lesson that life is not always fair, the value of paying attention to details, the importance of rooting for the underdog, the need to sometimes go with your gut, how teamwork counts, the joy of making an experience a family affair, the wisdom of valuing people of other races and ethnicities, and the way that life goes on in the face of defeat. All of these lessons have deep roots in both baseball and religion. But I think you get the idea, so I see no need to batter you with further commentary.

I want to close on a personal note, by telling you what the link between God, the Cubs and JRC has meant to me. What I intended to be a one-time reflection on God and the Cubs back at the Open Mike in 1984 has become something of a career and an obsession. In the process, these talks have become a small part of the rich tradition at JRC. While it's probably true that the High Holiday services would survive without them, why take that risk?

Of course, the talks, through the incredible teamwork of many JRC members, became the first book published by JRC, back in 1999. That book was celebrated in a quintessential JRC fashion, with a party in which grandstands were erected in the sanctuary and "Take Me Out to the Ball Game" was sung in Yiddish. A second edition was published in 2002 and the twenty-fifth anniversary of these talks will give rise to a Silver Anniversary edition, which will be out early next year, in time for Valentine's Day.

More importantly, though, *Is God a Cubs Fan?* paved the way for three other books from JRC Press. These publications have become part of the fabric and spirit of the congregation. They have showcased some of the talent and creativity of our members and, in the process, they've raised more than a few *shekels* to support JRC activities.

On a personal level, these Open Mike talks and resulting books have led to connections with JRC members and others that have been very important to me. They have also deepened my love of and appreciation for baseball, for Judaism and for JRC.

So, as I suggested earlier, there may well be something slightly sick about a 65-year old guy caring about whether the Cubs win or lose. But—sick or not—I want to declare to you today that I do care. Devoutly.

GLOSSARY

· ·

asher bahar banu who chose us

asher kervanu who drew us close

Akedah the Torah portion that includes the story of the binding of Isaac by Abraham

bar mitzvah ceremony in which 13-year old boy becomes an adult member of the Jewish community; the analogous female ceremony is the bat mitzvah

bashert meant to be

beit din a tribunal of rabbis convened as a Jewish court of law to decide cases brought before it, as, for example, to approve a conversion

bentch pray, chant

bimah raised platform, or stage

bochers guys, young men

bracha blessing

bris ritual circumcision

bubbelah term of endearment

chacham wise man

chai life, in Hebrew; in the Hebrew numbering system, the letters chayt and yod (that spell the word *chai*) represent the number eighteen

challah braided bread traditionally eaten on Sabbath

Chanukah Jewish winter holiday known as the Festival of Lights

chazan(im) cantor(s)

chutzpah nerve, hubris

daven pray

echad, shtayim, shalosh one, two, three

Eretz Yisrael land of Israel

erev eve of a holiday, begins at sundown

frum meticulously observant

gefilte fish stewed or baked fish stuffed with a mixture of the fish flesh, bread crumbs, eggs, and seasoning, or prepared as balls or oval cakes boiled in a fish stock

goyim; goyish non-Jews; not Jewish

hasidic belonging to a sect of Jews that developed in 18th-century Poland and Russia

Ha Shem a name for God—literally, The Name

hocking continually bothering

kippah (pl. kippot) skull cap(s) or yarmulke(s)

klezmer a type of traditional Jewish music

knish a small round or square of dough stuffed with a filling and baked or fried

Kol Nidre opening prayer of the evening service of *Yom Kippur*

kvell beam with pride

kvetch complain

l'hadlik ner shel Cubbelas to light the Cubs' candle

l'shanah ha ba-a b'Wrigley Field next year may we be in Wrigley Field

Leviticus the third book of the five books of Moses that make up the Torah

mashiach messiah

matzah unleavened bread eaten during Passover

mezzuzah (pl. mezzuzot) small container of scripture affixed to the door frames of Jewish homes *midrash (pl. midrashim)* story that expands on or explains a portion of Torah

mikva bath used in ritual purification and in conversion ceremonies

minhag(im) custom(s)

minyan group of at least ten Jews required for prayer; at JRC, the name of a group that meets each Saturday morning for services

mishigas silliness or an oddity

mishpocha family

mishuga crazy

nachas joy, pleasure

nosh snack

nu? so?

oy! oh!

oy-a-brach see *oy*

oy vey! oh no! (literally, oh, woe!)

parsha a portion of the Torah

Pesach the holiday that celebrates the deliverance of the Jews from slavery in Egypt; also called Passover

Rosh Hashanah the beginning of the year on the Jewish calendar

schlep drag or carry

schmutzig dirty

shabbat shalom good Sabbath (literally a *Sabbath of peace*), a greeting on the Sabbath

shabbos Sabbath

shalom hello (also means good-bye and peace)

Shana Tova Happy New Year

shanda shame

shehehianu traditional prayer of thanksgiving

shekel old Jewish coin, currency

shomer shabbos observant of religious tenets for the Sabbath

shul synagogue

Torah the five books of Moses

trayf unkosher food

tzedakah charity as a religious obligation

vay iz meer! my gosh! (literally, woe is me!)

Yid a person who speaks Yiddish, a Jew

Yiddish language spoken by Jews of Europe

Yom Kippur the holiest day of the Jewish year, ten days after Rosh Hashanah

yontiff holiday

BIOGRAPHIES

ARNIE KANTER attends the JRC *minyan* and Cubs games. In between, he consults to major law firms, works obsessively on Photoshop, and spends as much time as possible with his three granddaughters, Zoe, Phoebe, and Riley. Arnie has written a bunch of books, some serious and some humorous, but has difficulty determining which are which. His two daughters, Jodi and Wendy, have left the nest, so he lives in Evanston, Illinois, with his poet-psychotherapist wife, Carol, and their above-average standard poodle, Sosa.

DARLENE GROSSMAN is the older of twin girls born on a Sunday when the Cubs split a double header, prophetically losing the first game. She has a B.F.A. in graphic design from the University of Illinois, Urbana, and works for a textbook publisher. She also freelances and babysits for her grandchildren. Darlene shares an empty nest with her devoted husband, Ray, who cheers for that *other* Chicago team.

SAM EIFLING, a graduate of Northwestern University, has won national and regional journalism awards for writing about boxing, competitive eating, and hand-fishing of catfish. He began his writing career in 1998—coincidentally, the year he saw his first Cubs game.

ORDER FORM

● ●

To order additional copies of *Is God A Cubs Fan?* please fill
out the form below and send it with $14.95* plus $5.00 per
order for shipping and handling, to:

> IGCF, c/o JRC Press
> 303 Dodge Avenue
> Evanston, IL 60202-3252

Make check or money order payable to JRC.

Allow three weeks for delivery.

Number of copies: _____ x $14.95 each =$ _____

Add shipping & handling: $5 x _____ books = $_____

Total: $_____

Ship to: _____

Name: _____

Address: _____

City: _____

State: Zip Code: _____

Telephone: _____ / _____

E-Mail: _____

* please call for special rate on multiple copies: 847.328.7678